GREAT MOUNTAINS

A Visitor's Companion

George Wuerthner

Photographs by George Wuerthner
Illustrations by Douglas W. Moore

STACKPOLE BOOKS

0 11557 02498 2

Published by
STACKPOLE BOOKS
5067 Ritter Road
Mechanicsburg, PA 17055
www.stackpolebooks.com

Printed in China

10 9 8 7 6 5 4 3 2 1

First edition

Cover design by Caroline M. Stover
Cover photo by George Wuerthner

Library of Congress Cataloging-in-Publication Data
Wuerthner, George.
    Great Smoky Mountains : a visitor's companion / George
Wuerthner ; photographs by George Wuerthner ; illustrations by
Douglas W. Moore.—1st ed.
        p. cm.
    ISBN: 0–8117–2498–0
    1. Great Smoky Mountains National Park (N.C. and Tenn.)—
Guidebooks. 2. Natural history—Great Smoky Mountains National
Park (N.C. and Tenn.) I. Title.

F443.G7 W84 2003
917.68'890454—dc21   2002066886

917.68
WUER

CONTENTS

About the Author

George Wuerthner is a full-time freelance photographer, writer, and ecologist. An authority on national parks and conservation issues, he has written more than twenty other books, including the *Visitor's Companion* series of *Yellowstone, Yosemite, Grand Canyon, Olympic, Mount Rainier,* and *Rocky Mountain.* Other books include *Texas's Big Bend Country, California Wilderness Areas: Coasts and Mountains, Alaska Mountain Ranges, The Adirondacks: Forever Wild,* and *Oregon Wildflower Hikes.*

Wuerthner graduated from the Universtiy of Montana with degrees in wildlife biology and botany and received a master's degree in science writing from the University of California, Santa Cruz; his later academic training included graduate work in geography at the University of Oregon. He has worked as a university instructor, wilderness guide, park ranger, and biologist. Wuerthner currently lives in Eugene, Oregon, with his wife and two children.

Introduction

If you look at a road map of the southern United States, most of the region is crisscrossed by a spaghetti-like tangle of interstate highways and roads. But in the midst of this knot of pavement is one large area of undeveloped landscape lying along the spine of the southern Appalachian Mountains—Great Smoky Mountains National Park (GSMNP). The park is the premier wildlands in the southeastern United States and one of the greatest biological treasures of the entire national park system. Yet it is a restored wildlands. Much of the park was once logged, grazed by livestock, or farmed. But beginning in the 1920s, a movement to create a great natural area in the East culminated in the establishment of the park through the acquisition of private lands. Today, GSMNP stands as a symbol of the recuperative abilities of nature. Despite the annual deluge of people who descend upon these mountains, one can find a peaceful and beautiful sanctuary where natural processes and nature reign supreme.

The park encompasses about 520,000 acres, with some twenty summits higher than 6,000 feet, including Mount Guyot (6,621 feet) and Mount LeConte (6,593 feet). Even more remarkable, 36 miles of the crest is at or above 5,000 feet—the highest continuous stretch of land in the eastern United States. This is literally the rooftop of the East.

Although westerners, who are accustomed to mountains that rise 14,000 feet or more, may sneer at the notion that the East has any "high" mountains, the actual rise in elevation between lowlands and peaks in the Great Smoky Mountains is nearly as great as in many western ranges. Gatlinburg, Tennessee, lies at 1,250 feet above sea level, while the summit of Clingmans Dome is more than a mile higher at 6,643 feet. In the entire eastern United States, only 6,684-foot Mount Mitchell in the nearby Black Mountains is higher than Clingmans Dome. A hike from Gatlinburg to the summit takes one through climatic and plant zones

Springtime along Little Pigeon River. Great Smoky Mountains National Park preserves 520,000 acres and is one of the largest protected natural areas in the southeastern United States.

similar to those encountered on a walk from Georgia to Maine, yet it's possible for a dedicated hiker to make such a trek in one day in GSMNP. As one resident of the region described it: "Everywhere you go, it's climb, scramble, clamber down, and climb again. You can't go nowhere in this country without climbing both ways."

But elevation gain is only one of many superlatives found in the park. The Great Smoky Mountains straddle the North Carolina–Tennessee border and are a subrange of the southern Appalachian Mountains. The

Appalachians run parallel to the Atlantic Ocean all the way from Canada's Newfoundland to northern Alabama. Though the name is the same along the entire length, there is some variation among the rocks, reflecting the geological history. Geographers usually consider Pennsylvania the dividing line between the northern and southern Appalachians. A subdivision of this region is the Blue Ridge Province, which includes GSMNP.

The Smokies are extremely rugged and steep—carved by moving water. But unlike areas in New England, they were never glaciated during the ice ages. That has had several effects. Unlike much of the glaciated landscapes of Maine, New Hampshire, and elsewhere, there are no glacier-scoured natural lakes in these mountains. The advance of ancient glaciers

Gatlinburg, Tennessee, lies at 1,250 feet above sea level, while the summit of Clingmans Dome lies more than a mile higher at 6,643 feet. A hike from Gatlinburg to the summit would take you through climatic and plant zones similar to walking from Georgia to Maine, yet it's quite possible for a dedicated hiker to make such a trek in one day in the national park.

did, however, produce colder conditions that supported plant communities more typical of northern areas, such as the spruce-fir forests that are now isolated in the higher parts of the Smokies. These enclaves of northern plant communities allowed many northern wildlife species to colonize the region. The Great Smoky Mountains are often the southern limit for species that are relatively common farther north, such as the northern flying squirrel and the water shrew.

Compared with the northern Appalachian ranges—the White Mountains of New Hampshire and the Green Mountains of Vermont—the southern Appalachians, and the Great Smoky Mountains in particular, are exceedingly wet. The highest reaches of the park receive more than 90 inches of precipitation a year—rivaling the Pacific Northwest for moisture. The moisture in the air softens the vistas and contributes to the smoky haze that gives the range its name.

The heavy precipitation and deep soils support one of the most diverse forested landscapes in North America. Indeed, there are more species of trees in GSMNP than in all of northern Europe. It is also a center of diversity for salamanders, with at least 22 (some estimate as many as 29) species found in the park. The park also supports 1,500 species of flowering plants, 50 mammals, 200 birds, 80 reptiles and amphibians, and 70 fish.

Even though three-fourths of the land was cut over during its pre-park years, the Smokies still support the largest tract of virgin forest left in the eastern United States. In particular, the cove hardwood forests contain giant trees that rival the big conifers of the Pacific Northwest. And with park protection, the rest of the forest is slowly recovering some of its former splendor.

When a movement developed to create a national park in the southern Appalachians, not surprisingly, the Great Smoky Mountains were chosen. The park was authorized in 1926 and dedicated in 1940. Its scenic vistas and wildlands have made it one of the most popular national parks in the country, but its rich biological treasures helped gain its designation as a Biosphere Preserve in 1976 and a World Heritage Site in 1983.

Besides preserving the natural heritage of the southern Appalachian Mountains, GSMNP also seeks to interpret the cultural landscape. Cabins, barns, mills, churches, and other remnants of early human occupation are preserved and maintained, providing insight into the human story as well. In particular, Cades Cove and Cataloochee host many buildings and sites from the pre-park era.

Dogwood in bloom at Cades Cove. Great Smoky Mountains National Park is recognized worldwide as a center for biodiversity. The park was named a Biosphere Preserve in 1976 and a World Heritage Site in 1983 and preserves 1,500 species of flowering plants, 50 mammals, 200 birds, 80 reptiles and amphibians, and 70 fish.

GSMNP also protects one of the largest tracts of wildlands in the eastern United States. That is, most of the park is dominated by self-regulating and self-generating natural processes. Rivers are not dammed to control floods. Predators are not killed to protect prey species. On a landscape scale, this is one of the few areas in the eastern United States where such natural processes are free to operate with minimal direct interference from humans.

In addition to protecting the region's natural features, GSMNP also attempts to interpret the human history of the area through the restoration and preservation of the area's pioneering history such as displayed at the Oconaluftee Pioneer Village.

Despite this management policy by the National Park Service, GSMNP is still affected by human activities. Acid rainfall resulting from power generation is slowly degrading the water and plant communities of the park. Exotic species of plants, insects, diseases, and animals introduced by accident or on purpose threaten the park's biodiversity and are contributing to its impoverishment. Global warming may soon eliminate plant communities such as the spruce-fir forest. Protecting the park from these threats is not an easy task.

Great Smoky Mountains Geography

The Great Smoky Mountains form the Tennessee–North Carolina border. A number of rivers and creeks have their headwaters within the park. Starting just south and west of Bryson City along the park's southern border is the Tuckasegee, which drains into Little Tennessee River. The Tennessee Valley Authority (TVA) dammed the river to create Fontana Lake. On the southwest lies Abrams Creek, which drains Cades Cove and flows into Chilhowee Lake, another TVA reservoir. The north slope is drained by Little River and Little Pigeon River; Little Pigeon River flows past Gatlinburg. On the north lies Crosby Creek, and across the divide from Crosby Creek is Big Creek. On the northeast lies Cataloochee Creek. Draining the southeastern slope of the Smokies toward Cherokee, North Carolina, is the Oconaluftee River. Each major drainage has unique aspects that make it worth visiting. Following is a brief overview of park geography and major subregions.

Abrams Creek and Cades Cove

Abrams Creek drains Cades Cove, Tennessee, the most famous part of the park. A paved loop road circles the cove, providing access to its many features, including a number of restored or maintained cabins, churches,

The mountain rimmed valley known as Cades Cove is the most famous part of the park. A paved loop road circles the cove providing access to its many features, including quite a number of restored or maintained structures such as cabins, churches, mills, and other buildings. Geologically, the cove is made of limestone exposed by the erosion of overlying rock strata. This limestone produced fertile soils, which contributed to the early settlement of the valley.

Abrams Creek drains Cades Cove and is named for Old Abrams, a Cherokee chief.

mills, and other buildings. The cove is really a valley entirely surrounded by mountains. Geologically, the cove is made of limestone exposed by the erosion of overlying rock strata. This limestone produced fertile soils and contributed to the early settlement of the valley. Abrams Creek, which drains the entire cove and is one of the major streams in the park, is named for Old Abrams, a Cherokee chief of mixed blood.

John Oliver and his family were the first white residents of the cove and settled in the valley in 1818, while the area was still legally part of the Cherokee territory. Other families followed in 1821 and throughout the 1820s. At one time there were three schools and seven churches in the valley. Just prior to the creation of the park, the cove supported up to 100 families numbering upward of 700 people. The east end of the cove was heavily logged while under the control of the Little River Lumber Company and is still recovering from past timber-cutting practices.

Tremont

The Tremont area lies along the West and Middle Prongs of Little River on the Tennessee side of the Smoky Divide. Dripping Spring Mountain, Thunderhead Mountain, and Bote Mountain all enclose this area. Tremont was the name given to a logging camp operated by the Little River Lumber Company, based on the abundance of trees in the area. Today, the Great Smoky Mountains Institute operates a camp at Tremont.

Elkmont

Elkmont lies on Little River on the Tennessee side of the mountains. It was originally a logging camp established in 1901 by the Little River Lumber Company. The lands surrounding Elkmont were sold to the government in 1926, making them some of the first lands purchased for the eventual creation of GSMNP. Today, Elkmont hosts a ranger station and the park's largest campground.

Greenbrier

Greenbrier lies on Little Pigeon River on the Tennessee side of the park. In pre-park days, it was one of the more settled areas, with a school, several churches, and two stores. The Smoky Mountain Hiking Club built a cabin here in 1934; it is now a historic structure. Despite its popularity with early settlers, today Greenbrier is one of the least visited parts of the park.

Cosby

Cosby Creek drains the northeastern part of GSMNP. It was named for Dr. James Cosby, one of the first doctors to reside in the region. The wide but isolated basin was once known as the "moonshiner's capital." One of the best examples of old-growth virgin forest in GSMNP is found in

Albright Grove on Indian Creek. Also accessible via Cosby is the trail to Mount Cammerer. The 360-degree view from the fire tower on Mount Cammerer is one of the best in the park.

Big Creek

The Big Creek watershed drains the northeast end of GSMNP in North Carolina. The area was logged by the Crestmont Lumber Company between 1909 and 1918. One of the largest trees ever cut in the region came from this drainage. One logger claimed that it was more than 12 feet in diameter. A large village and lumber camp were located in the lower end of the drainage. During the 1930s, a Civilian Conservation Corps camp operated in the valley.

Cataloochee

Tucked in the northeastern corner of GSMNP lies the Cataloochee Valley. Although the area is considered remote today, it once housed the largest community in the Smokies, with an estimated 1,200 people scattered up and down the valley. At one time the Park Service contemplated increasing development in this valley, but it never happened. Today, it's considered one of the "forgotten" valleys, where visitors can travel at a slower pace and with fewer crowds.

Raven Fork

Raven Fork, a tributary of the Oconaluftee River, lies upstream from the Cherokee Indian Reservation in North Carolina. It was named for Cherokee chief Kalanu, which means "raven." Although a loop road travels up the drainage, it remains one of the least developed areas in the park. The Raven Fork watershed is defined by Balsam Mountain on the east and Hughes Ridge on the west. The Balsam Mountains are part of a connecting range that links the Great Smoky Mountains with the Blue Ridge Mountains to the east.

Oconaluftee

The Oconaluftee River is one of the major drainages on the North Carolina side of the mountains. The name is a corruption of an Indian term that means "villages by the river." The river starts at Newfound Gap and flows toward Smokemont along an old fault line. The river basin is defined by Mount Kephart and Thomas Divide on the west; Hughes

The Raven Fork seen here was named for Cherokee Chief Kalanu, which means "raven." Although a loop road travels up the drainage, it remains one of the least developed areas in the park.

Ridge separates it from the Raven Fork drainage. The Oconaluftee Valley was settled earlier than was the Tennessee side of the mountains. As early as 1790, the Mingus and Hughes families were farming the fertile river bottoms there. Other early settlers, including the Hyatts, Becks, Bradleys, and Enloes, all left their names on physical features in the area.

The Oconaluftee River starts at Newfound Gap and flows toward Smokemont along an old fault line. The Oconaluftee Valley was settled earlier than was the Tennessee side of the mountains.

Although these settlers used the rest of the mountains for timber, hunting, and grazing, most of their farming was concentrated in the valley bottoms. Development of the uplands changed in 1917, when the Champion Fiber Company acquired land in the drainage and logged the basin all the way to Newfound Gap. A mill was established at Smokemont, and a small village grew up around it. Acquisition of the Champion lands in this drainage was a major factor in the creation of GSMNP. Today, Newfound Gap Road provides access to the drainage, as well as to a campground, picnic areas, and trails.

Deep Creek

Deep Creek drains into the Tuckasegee River near Bryson City, North Carolina. Noland Divide and Thomas Divide define the drainage borders.

At one time, the Bryson family, for whom Bryson City is named, operated a lodge on Deep Creek. A wagon road connected the lodge with the city. During the logging era, splash dams were created on Deep Creek and its tributaries. Then, when heavy rains swelled the streams, the dams were dynamited, sending the logs downstream to the mills.

Noland and Forney Creeks

To the west of Deep Creek are Noland and Forney Creeks. Both valleys once supported significant human populations, but today, they are among the wildest drainages in the park. Noland Creek is accessed by North Shore Road out of Bryson City. Forney Creek is one of the major roadless valleys in the park and is accessible only by trail off Clingmans Dome Road or by boat across Fontana Lake. Families that once farmed the Forney Creek Valley include the Welches and the Coles.

Like elsewhere in the Smokies, logging of the slopes began just after the turn of the century. From 1909 to 1920, the Norwood Lumber Company

The Smokies, seen here by Deep Creek, are extremely rugged and steep. But unlike mountains farther north in New England, which were gouged by glaciers, the Smokies were shaped primarily by moving water.

removed virtually all the larger trees from the valley. This was followed by a major fire, fueled in part by logging slash.

Hazel Creek

Draining the North Carolina slope of the Smokies, Hazel Creek flows into Fontana Reservoir near Fontana Village. Its headwaters lie near Silers Bald along the Appalachian Trail. Prior to the establishment of the park, Hazel Creek was the site of heavy logging. For several decades, the Ritter Lumber Company cut forests in the drainage, removing most of the salable timber. Proctor, a logging camp on Hazel Creek, once had more than a thousand residents. A trail now runs up the valley, and relicts of the old logging grade extend for miles up the valley.

CLIMATE

The southern Appalachian Mountains are a formidable barrier to the movement of air masses across the continent. The Great Smoky Mountains, constituting one of the highest subranges in the southern Appalachians, exert a tremendous influence on regional weather and climatic patterns. The mountains on the eastern slope are affected by air masses coming from the Atlantic Ocean, while the western flanks have a climate more typical of the interior of the continent. To fully understand how climate plays out in the park, we have to look at regional weather patterns.

Regional Climatic Patterns

In general, compared with other spruce-fir forests in Canada or northern New England, the higher-elevation forests of the southern Appalachian Mountains are wetter and experience less severe temperatures. Only along the coast of Maine and New Brunswick or in the Pacific Northwest is it as wet or as mild as in the southern Appalachians.

During a typical summer, the Bermuda high strongly influences weather in the park. It funnels warm, moist air from the South Atlantic Ocean into the southeastern United States. High-pressure systems tend to create stable, often stagnant air conditions dominated by sunny weather. It is exactly these regional conditions, with their high humidity and haze, that create the bluish cast for which the Smokies are named.

In winter, conditions in the park change dramatically. Winter storms from the Gulf of Mexico track inland along the lower Mississippi and encounter the western slope of the Smokies, dumping large quantities of rain and occasionally snow, particularly at higher elevations. Nevertheless, the heaviest rainfall typically arrives via storms off the South Atlantic. These storms move inland and drop their moisture on the eastern flanks of the mountains. While most summer moisture comes in the form of short

Winter storms from the Gulf of Mexico track inland along the lower Mississippi and encounter the western slope of the Smokies where they dump large quantities of rain and occasionally snow, particularly at higher elevations as seen here along the crest of the Smokies.

but intense thundershowers, winter brings major frontal storms that can last for days.

Another factor that influences climate is the distance from oceanic water sources—in this case, the Gulf of Mexico or the South Atlantic. Not surprisingly, the farther inland one goes, the lower the precipitation amounts. Asheville, North Carolina, for instance, averages 45 inches of annual precipitation, while Blairsville, Georgia, south of GSMNP but closer to the moisture sources, receives 56 inches of precipitation a year.

Precipitation also increases as one ascends the mountain slopes, due to the cooling effect of altitude on air masses. Cool air holds less moisture than warm air, and as air masses move up a mountain slope, they drop most of their moisture load. Precipitation at park headquarters near

Gatlinburg, Tennessee, at 1,460 feet, is typically 55 to 56 inches. Precipitation amounts increase until approximately 5,000 feet, where they level off. The higher elevations in GSMNP typically receive as much as 80 to 90 inches of annual precipitation, and sometimes in excess of 100 inches.

Just to put this into perspective, "rainy" Seattle, Washington, receives only 37 inches of annual precipitation, and Port Angeles, on the "wet" Olympic Peninsula adjacent to Olympic National Park, seems almost arid by comparison, with only 29 inches of annual precipitation. Clearly, the

Rainy day along the Little River. The Smokies often receive in excess of 90 inches or more of precipitation, making them one of the wettest places in the United States, second only to the wettest parts of the Pacific Northwest and coastal Alaska.

southern Appalachians easily qualify as one of the wettest places in the country, with only a few areas in the Pacific Northwest and coastal Alaska receiving more annual precipitation.

One difference between the Pacific Northwest and the southern Appalachians has to do with the annual distribution of precipitation. The Pacific Northwest enjoys nearly rain-free summer months, with the majority of precipitation falling in the winter. In contrast, precipitation in the southern Appalachians is evenly distributed throughout the year, with most places averaging a minimum of 4 inches a month.

Cloudy days often dominate the southern Appalachians in the summer months, with fall and winter recording the greatest number of clear days. For example, Asheville, just north and east of the park, typically records only four or five clear days during July and August. Much of the cloudiness is due to the development of thunderheads in the afternoons, with an average of twelve to thirteen thunderstorms occurring each month during July and August. Mornings, however, are often sunny. Even though overcast days are the norm, rainfall doesn't dominate in the summer months; only one in four days is actually rainy. Throughout the summer, periods of dry weather lasting four or more days can be expected.

The reason for this is that while stable high-pressure systems generally dominate, the daily rising of hot air over the mountains causes clouds to form. The sun heats the air during the morning; the rising air then condenses as it rises over the cooler higher elevations of the mountains, creating clouds and often thunderstorms.

Compared with the western United States and more continental climates, the temperature variation between day and night is not great. The large amounts of moisture in the air (contributing to the humidity), combined with the frequent cloud cover, work to insulate the mountains from large temperature swings. Often only 10 to 15 degrees separates the high for the afternoon and the nighttime low. However, up to 30 degrees may separate the range of temperatures throughout the seasons.

There is a decrease in temperature as one climbs up the mountains. The spruce-fir forests above 5,000 feet are typically 10 to 15 degrees cooler than the surrounding lowlands.

Seasonal temperature trends also vary with elevation. There is a gradual warming between January and March, and spring is evident at all lower elevations by April. This is delayed by about a month at higher elevations, and spring does not arrive at Newfound Gap until the beginning of May.

The Chimneys area on a rainy day. The Great Smoky Mountains as one of the highest ranges in the eastern United States create a formidable barrier to the movement of air masses. The eastern slope is affected by air masses coming from the Atlantic Ocean, while the western flanks have a more continental climate typical of the interior of the continent.

Spruce forest with maple in fog near Balsam Mountain. Compared to other spruce-fir forest regimes found across Canada or even in northern New England, the higher elevation forests of the southern Appalachian Mountains are wetter and experience less severe temperatures. Only the spruce-fir forests found along the coast of Maine and in the Pacific Northwest experience a similarly wet and mild climate.

Similarly, winterlike conditions arrive at the highest elevations by late October but are delayed until November at the lowest elevations.

The Seasons

Springtime weather is variable. Freezing temperatures often occur at night, but mid-April daytime temperatures can reach the seventies and sometimes the eighties. By May, daytime temperatures in the eighties are more common, and nighttime lows are in the forties and fifties. Rainfall averages between 4 and 4.5 inches a month during April and May.

Summers are hot and humid—at least at the lower elevations. Afternoon thunderstorms are common. Temperatures reach the nineties during the day and fall to the sixties and seventies at night. However, just about perfect temperatures can be found at the highest elevations, such as Clingmans Dome, where the highest temperature ever recorded was 80 degrees.

Autumn brings the clearest skies. Daytime temperatures are often in the seventies and eighties, but nighttime temperatures fall to the fifties and sixties. Freezing temperatures are common at night by November. This is the driest time of year.

Autumn color of red maple leaves. The annual fall color spectacle accounts for some of the highest visitation periods in the park.

Winter months tend to be cool, even cold at times. Temperatures at the lower elevations reach a high in the fifties about half the time, but night-time temperatures are typically at or below freezing. Up to 2 feet of snow can fall in the higher mountains, but it usually doesn't last more than a few days before melting.

WEATHER CHART

Gatlinburg, Tennessee (elevation 1,462 feet)

Month	Average High Temperature (°F)	Average Low Temperature (°F)	Precipitation (inches)
January	51	28	4.8
February	54	29	4.8
March	61	34	5.3
April	71	42	4.5
May	79	50	4.5
June	86	58	5.2
July	88	59	5.7
August	87	60	5.3
September	83	55	3.0
October	73	43	3.1
November	61	33	3.4
December	52	28	4.5

Clingmans Dome (elevation 6,643 feet)

Month	Average High Temperature (°F)	Average Low Temperature (°F)	Precipitation (inches)
January	35	19	7.0
February	35	18	8.2
March	39	24	8.2
April	49	34	6.5
May	57	43	6.0
June	63	49	6.9
July	65	53	8.3
August	64	52	6.8
September	60	47	5.1
October	53	38	5.4
November	42	28	6.4
December	37	21	7.3

HISTORY

The Great Smoky Mountains are among the most rugged and highest terrain in the southeastern United States. These mountains have been a barrier to human travel and endeavors for centuries. People largely flowed around the mountains, settled on their fringes, and were unwilling or unable to exploit their resources. The area that now makes up Great Smoky Mountains National Park has nevertheless played a role in both the regional history and the conservation history of the United States.

The First Humans

The southern Appalachian Mountains have been home to people for thousands of years. The human pageant that has unfolded there is, as they say, "as old as the hills." The Paleo-Indians were the first known human presence. These big-game hunters entered the southeastern United States by 9000 BC in the post-Pleistocene era, following the retreat of ice-age glaciers from the North American continent. They moved around ceaselessly in the quest for game, focusing on large mammals such as mammoths and bison and perhaps even driving some species extinct. The Paleo-Indians were gradually replaced by the Archaic culture, but it is unknown whether the Archaic people were direct descendants of the Paleo-Indians. The Archaic people had a more diversified diet that included small game, fish, and various plant materials, and, unlike the roving bands of Paleo-Indians, they were more sedentary, moving from seasonal camp to seasonal camp within a defined territory. Even as early as 8000 BC, these people had set up trade routes that brought copper from the upper Midwest and shells from the Gulf of Mexico to camps along the Tennessee River and tributaries that flow from the southern Appalachian Mountains.

The next step in cultural development was agriculture. The new cultural advance was known as the woodland tradition. People began to

Looking north from Clingmans Dome. At 6,643 feet, it is the highest peak in Tennessee. The Great Smoky Mountains contain twenty summits higher than 6,000 feet and are among the most rugged terrain in southeastern United States.

domesticate plants, and the new food resources led to the development of villages, the construction of mounds and other earthworks, and the production of ceramic pots and other earthenware. Up until the late woodland era, all hunting was done with spears or atlatls. The development of the bow and arrow approximately 2,000 years ago greatly increased hunting efficiency. Corn imported by trade with Mexico, along with other crops, became a mainstay of the diet. By AD 1000, these farming cultures had developed a large population base with a well-organized hierarchical structure, particularly in the Ohio and Mississippi Valleys. By AD 1400, these people had adopted a valley-bottom farming culture with compact, fortified towns dominated by a central plaza where religious ceremonies were conducted. Trade with regions as far away as the Rockies and even Central America occurred throughout this period. This culture was still developing and changing when the first Europeans entered the Southeast around 1500.

During this entire period of human occupation and cultural flux, people adapted to changing conditions of climate and technological advances. They migrated from place to place, seeking better conditions or merely in response to the pressures brought by wealthier or more numerous neighbors. Some anthropologists speculate that growing warfare was sapping the vitality of these cultures at the time of European contact.

One thing is certain, it is unlikely that any Indian people persisted in the same location for thousands of years. Indeed, the evidence suggests that the major tribes, such as the Creek, Choctaw, Chickasaw, and others encountered by Hernando de Soto, the first European to venture into the Southeast during the mid-1500s, were relatively recent immigrants or invaders themselves. These groups had moved to the Southeast from the North perhaps only a few generations before the Spanish and others began to explore and colonize the region.

The Cherokee

At the time of European exploration and settlement of the GSMNP region, the Cherokee people controlled the river valleys of western North Carolina and eastern Tennessee. Although there is no evidence that the Cherokee actually lived in what is now GSMNP, they did hunt and travel throughout the region. The Cherokee figure prominently in the history of the southern Appalachians. Members of the tribe still reside in the area, and a reservation exists immediately east of the park border.

The Cherokee are related to the Iroquois people of New York. The best guess is that they split from this group and gradually moved southward, occupying the GSMNP region by 1500 if not earlier. The Cherokee territory stretched from the Ohio River in the north into South Carolina, but the majority of their villages were found along the Tennessee River and its tributaries, near what is now the tristate Tennessee–North Carolina–Georgia border. There were three main groups within the tribe, each with its own dialect. The lower villages were located along the headwaters of the Savannah River in Georgia and South Carolina; the overhill towns were in eastern Tennessee, along the lower reaches of the Little Tennessee River and its tributaries the Tellico and Hiwassee; and the middle towns were in western North Carolina, at the headwaters of the Little Tennessee and Tuckasegee Rivers. The Great Smoky Mountains were at the heart of their territory.

The typical Cherokee lived in a small village of perhaps fifty to sixty dwellings located in the rich bottomlands, where they farmed corn, beans, squash, and tobacco and, after contact with Europeans, even grew fruit such as apples. Men hunted the surrounding mountains for bear, deer, turkey, and other game. Home was a wooden cabin made from logs, notched on the end to hold the building together, with a bark roof, a door, and no windows. Smoke from the central campfire escaped through a hole in the roof. In the center of the village was the council house, a large building that could accommodate several hundred people. Festivals and spiritual ceremonies were held in the council house.

The Cherokee organized their lives around clans, with relatively equal status accorded to all tribal members. Clan kinship was determined by the mother's side of the family. From all accounts, the Cherokee spent a great deal of time in warfare, and most status within the tribe was achieved by exploits on the battlefield.

De Soto encountered a number of Cherokee villages on his march across the Southeast in 1540. Most of these encounters were uneventful, but on one occasion, his soldiers were given a bison skin, which was described as "an ox hide as thin as a calf's skin, and the hair like a soft wool between the coarse and fine wool of sheep." It was likely the first recorded report of bison in the New World. Bison once ranged as far south as northern Florida and were found throughout the western portion of the Carolinas, Tennessee, and elsewhere.

Soon after de Soto's travels through the region, the Spanish established forts and colonies in St. Augustine, Florida, and a few other locations on the coast. From these posts, occasional Spanish military exploration and trading parties ventured into the foothills of the mountains, where they no doubt encountered the Cherokee.

The first contact with English settlers and traders did not occur until the 1670s. In 1673, English traders James Needham and Gabriel Arthur traveled to the Cherokee's overhills capital of Chota to establish trade ties. Needham described the village as being surrounded by palisades, built to protect it from warring tribes that lived downriver. Needlam left the village and returned to Virginia, but Arthur stayed behind to learn the language. Disguised as a Cherokee, Arthur accompanied the chief of Chota on war parties and raids against enemies as far away as the Shawnee villages along the Ohio River and south to the Spanish settlements in Florida. In one raid against the Shawnee, Arthur was captured and taken prisoner, but he was released when it was discovered that he was a white man. After traveling back to the Cherokee villages, Arthur returned to Virginia.

Contact between whites and the Cherokee continued throughout the late 1600s and into the 1700s. By all accounts, the major occupation of male Cherokee was warfare and raiding. Through war exploits, a young Cherokee gained status in the tribe. It even affected romantic aspirations. A successful young brave was invariably viewed as a good catch by the young women of the tribe, who actively courted well-known and celebrated warriors.

Although intertribal warfare was common, and disputes and battles even occurred between the major clans of the Cherokee tribe, the coming of Europeans helped fuel these conflicts. Long before whites began to settle in the region, directly competing with the Cherokee for land and resources, trade in European goods helped increase the level of tribal conflict. Since success in warfare was such a central part of the Cherokee culture, the advantages of European arms did not go unnoticed. The desire to obtain firearms and other European goods fueled an "arms race" among the tribes. Each tribe sought to garner more and newer weapons. They paid for these goods by killing and trapping wildlife and exchanging the furs for trade items. As wildlife populations were depleted near the villages, tribes expanded their efforts outward, inevitably coming into conflict with their neighbors, who in turn were trying to obtain their own furs for trade by the same means.

Besides increasing the level of warfare and raids of retribution among the tribes, trade with the Europeans contributed to a growing Indian slave trade. The South Carolina colony, established in 1670, began to accept not only furs and meat in trade but also prisoners of war. These prisoners were sold as slaves. The Cherokee soon adopted slavery themselves and legally held slaves up through the Civil War.

The English were not the only Europeans colonizing the Southeast. By the early 1700s, the French had established bases in the region, including Fort Toulouse near what is today Montgomery, Alabama. Worried that the French might try to pitch the Cherokee against them, the English sought to solidify relations. Sir Alexander Cuming traveled to Cherokee towns to negotiate with the tribe and garner its loyalty to the crown.

Several prominent Cherokee tribal members then accompanied Cuming to England, where they met the king and swore allegiance to Britain. In exchange, the Cherokee received more guns, ammunition, and other supplies.

Although relations between the English and the Cherokee were primarily businesslike, with limited conflict, the presence of the Europeans took its toll. Like other native people, the Cherokee were decimated by European diseases. As early as 1738, if not earlier, smallpox swept through the tribe, killing off an estimated half of the population. The loss of tribal members further upset regional power structures. Whether a tribe was suffering from disease at a particular point in time could greatly affect the outcome of conflicts. In 1715, the Cherokee drove the Shawnee northward out of the Cumberland River region. They continued their hereditary war with the Creeks (Muskogee) and fought an eleven-year war with the Chickasaw until the Chickasaw were ultimately defeated in 1768.

The encroaching westward movement of the English continued to antagonize the Cherokee, so when the French and Indian War began, the Cherokee sided with the French. A new treaty between the Cherokee and English was signed in 1754, however, reaffirming their alliance. It also provided for the construction of British military outposts in Cherokee territory.

Despite these seemingly positive trends, conflicts between the English and the Cherokee continued. Tensions escalated into open warfare after a number of young Cherokee captured some free-roaming horses that belonged to Virginia colonists. The outraged colonists attacked and killed twenty Indians; the scalps of the fallen warriors were turned in for bounty. These events provoked reprisals by the Cherokee. Eventually, the colonists declared war on the Cherokee, and a force of 1,600 whites attacked the Indians, destroying many villages. In 1760, the Cherokee attacked Fort Loudoun in retaliation, capturing the fort, killing some whites, and ransoming others. By the time France and England made peace in 1763, the tribes throughout the region had been devastated by warfare, loss of crops and orchards, and another smallpox epidemic. Although King George declared that the Blue Ridge Divide was the limit for settlement, immigrants began to flood across the mountains and into Cherokee territory to take advantage of weakened Indian resistance.

The continual movement of whites to the frontier and into lands claimed by the Cherokee only worsened the relationship between the two groups. When the Revolutionary War broke out in 1776, the Cherokee decided to join the British in war against the colonies. The British offered arms and ammunition to the Cherokee and paid them for colonists' scalps. In the end, the colonies mounted effective campaigns against the Cherokee, resulting in yet another treaty and loss of land for the tribe, including all the land east of the Blue Ridge. Treaty after treaty followed. By 1819, the Cherokee had signed their twenty-first treaty with the whites, ceding their last claim to what is now the Great Smoky Mountains.

Still, these concessions were not enough. The ever-growing colonial populations needed and demanded more land. The Indians were in the way, and many of the settlers wanted to get rid of them. The growing hostility toward the Indians along the frontier soon had a champion in Washington, D.C. Andrew Jackson, a war hero and Indian fighter, was elected president in 1828. Jackson basically ignored all previous treaties and permitted whites to freely invade Cherokee lands. He also allowed Georgia to extend state law to include the Cherokee Nation, negating Cherokee sovereignty. Georgia passed an act that confiscated all Cherokee lands, forbade testimony by Indians against white men, and distributed Indian lands to white settlers. After gold was discovered in northern Georgia within what was Cherokee territory, the pressure mounted for removal of the tribe from its homeland, and Jackson was more than happy to accommodate. At Jackson's urging, Congress passed the Indian Removal Act of 1830. Jackson expressed a perspective that was common at the time when he wrote, "[the Indian Removal Act] will place a dense and civilized population in large tracts of country now occupied by a few savage hunters."

Though popular with most frontiersman, not everyone in Congress supported Jackson or the Removal Act. One of the act's staunchest opponents was Congressman Davy Crockett of Tennessee. He called the action "unjust, dishonest, cruel, and short-sighted in the extreme." For his unpopular stance in defense of the Cherokee, he lost his bid for reelection and eventually left the state, moving west to Texas. Crockett later died at the battle of the Alamo.

Jackson, though eager to open Cherokee lands to white settlement, tried to rationalize his position by arguing that the Indian Removal Act would ultimately benefit the Indians as well. He said that the act

> will separate the Indians from immediate contact with settlements of whites; free them from the power of the States; enable them to pursue happiness in their own way and under their own rude

institutions; will retard the progress of decay, which is lessening their numbers, and perhaps cause them gradually, under the protection of the Government and through the influence of good counsels, to cast off their savage habits and become an interesting, civilized, and Christian community.

Apparently, the Cherokee did not agree with Jackson's perspective on the humanitarian benefits of the act. The Cherokee challenged its legality and took their case all the way to the U.S. Supreme Court. The Court threw out the case, claiming that the Cherokee people were not a sovereign nation and therefore had no legal basis for challenging the act.

Several missionaries living among the Cherokee refused to recognize Georgia's authority over the tribe and were promptly sentenced to four years' hard labor in the state penitentiary for refusing to take an oath of allegiance to the state. One of these missionaries took his case to the Supreme Court in *Worcester v. Georgia*. A year after annulling the tribe's authority and right to exist, the Court reversed itself and ruled in favor of the Cherokee as a sovereign people, thus invalidating the Removal Act. Justice John Marshall declared the forced removal of the Cherokee Nation illegal and unconstitutional. President Jackson ignored the Court and belligerently challenged Marshall's authority, declaring, "John Marshall has made his decision; let him enforce it now if he can."

To sidestep the issue and avoid a constitutional crisis, Jackson found a small number of Cherokee who were willing to sign a new treaty that basically agreed to the terms of the Removal Act. Although more than 16,000 Cherokee signed a petition voicing their opposition to the new treaty, they were ignored. Congress soon approved the treaty, and the Cherokee were ordered to move from their homes to the newly created Indian Territory in Oklahoma. In 1838, the army gathered up between 16,000 and 20,000 Cherokee at gunpoint and forced them to march from the Appalachians to the Oklahoma Territory. Some 2,000 Cherokee died en route on what became known as the "Trail of Tears."

Not all the Cherokee lost their homes or left the Appalachians. A number of tribal members were allowed to stay in the East under terms of an 1819 treaty; others fled from the solders and hid out in the hills, avoiding capture. In these mountain recesses, they suffered from the cold and a lack of food, living as fugitives. Eventually, all these people were allowed to remain in their ancestral homeland. As a result, a minimum of 1,100 Cherokee remained in the East after the general removal action was completed. William Thomas, a white man, who was an adopted Cherokee and later became a North Carolina state senator, was a champion and leader of the eastern band. Through his efforts, more than 50,000 acres of land were purchased on behalf of the Cherokee in North Carolina; this was the nucleus for what is now the Qualla Band Reservation. In 1868, Congress recognized the eastern band as a distinct and separate tribe from the western Cherokee in Oklahoma.

White Settlement

White expansion into western North Carolina and west of the Appalachians accelerated after the Revolutionary War. Some of the white settlement was spurred by land grants made by the colonies to soldiers as payment for their participation in the war effort; the rest was mostly a reflection of the ceaseless search for new lands and opportunities. By 1795, Tennessee had a population of 77,632 and was soon admitted into the Union as the sixteenth state. John Sevier, for whom Sevierville is

Hay fields in Cades Cove. Most of the early settlers of the Smokies lived on small subsistence farms. The cove communities generally prospered until 1850 when there were 132 families totaling 685 people living in the valley.

named, was elected governor. An old Indian fighter and expansionist, Sevier argued until his dying day for the removal of Indians from the region east of the Mississippi. Andrew Jackson was elected the state's first congressman.

Settlers from Tennessee pushed deeper into the mountains looking for land. Eventually, they made their way into the headwaters of the Little Pigeon River, setting up homes and farms in the fertile mountain valleys of Wears Cove, Tuckaleechee Cove, and Cades Cove. The overall rugged terrain on the North Carolina side of the Great Smoky Mountains was a greater barrier to settlement, and the human population was far less dense, although the region was settled earlier. In 1795, John Mingus and Ralph Hughes had settled on the Oconaluftee. Other settlers soon followed, clearing land and farming Raven Fork, Deep Creek, Forney Creek, and other North Carolina slope valleys.

Among the first settlers in Cades Cove were John Oliver and William Tipton, whose descendants were still living in the mountains when GSMNP was created. The Olivers were the first settlers; they moved into Cades Cove in 1818, a year before the Cherokee actually relinquished

Settlement was earlier on the North Carolina side of the mountains. Mingus Mill was built by John Mingus, who settled on the Oconaluftee in 1795.

John Oliver cabin, Cades Cove. The first white settler in Cades Cove was John Oliver and his family. They arrived in the cove in 1818.

control of the Smokies. For several years, they were the only people living in the cove, but after 1821, a number of other families, including the Jobes, Gregorys, Sparkes, and Cables, joined them. Their names are still evident in the park in such places as Gregory Bald, Sparks Lane, Cable Branch, Tipton Sugar Cove Branch, and Oliver Branch.

The community of Cades Cove slowly grew. An iron forge and the Cades Cove Baptist Church were both established in 1827—less than ten years after the first settler entered the valley. Cades Cove was becoming a viable community.

The life of the mountaineers was anything but easy, and poverty was widespread. Women were treated as little more than beasts of burden. They did much of the drudge work, including hoeing gardens, cutting firewood, and washing clothes, as well as caring for the children. According to Horace Kephart, the average mountaineer considered "his woman" to be "little more than a sort of superior domestic animal." Women married early, typically by the time they were fifteen or sixteen, and spent much of their adult life tending to children, since the typical woman bore seven to ten children.

Cades Cove Baptist Church was established in 1827, scarcely ten years after the first settlers arrived in Cades Cove. Most mountain residents were members of the Baptist church.

Isolated as they were by high mountains, bad roads, and dense forests, the settlers in these valleys were largely self-sufficient. Everyone farmed for a living, and nearly everything from oxen yokes to children's clothing was handmade. The first chore that all new settlers faced was creating farmland from forest. They chopped down all the smaller trees and girdled the larger ones to kill them. Fallen trees were burned on the site, adding their ashes to the soil as fertilizer. Like the Indians, the whites' major crop was corn. In addition, wheat, rye, barley, beans, pumpkins, apples, and other fruits and vegetables were grown. Chickens, pigs, sheep, and a few cows were also raised and killed for food. The settlers supplemented their fare with deer and bear, plus small game, and they gathered bushels of the abundant chestnuts.

The cove residents frequented the grassy balds that dotted the higher peaks to graze their livestock, at times spending weeks in the high pastures. At least some of these balds seem to be man-made. John Oliver stated that in the 1830s, James Spence cleared and burned what is now known as Spence Bald. No doubt other balds were expanded, if not created, by such activities. Grazing by animals helped to keep them open. Ace Sparks recalls that his father grazed as many as 700 cattle on Spence Bald in the 1890s.

Like in other places on the frontier, the population rose and fell in response to opportunities elsewhere. In 1830, when the Cherokee's land claims were invalidated in Georgia, some Cades Cove residents, including most of the Tiptons, moved away, looking for new opportunities to the south. When lands in the West became available for settlement, some cove residents headed to Missouri, Oregon, and elsewhere. However, with good lands and some new residents, the cove communities generally prospered until 1850, when there were 132 families totaling 685 people living in the valley. But due to changing economies and growing opportunities in the West, the population began to slide downward. By 1860, the population was just 275. But as families continued to have more children, the population gradually rose. There was a tremendous reduction in the diversity of families, however. In 1850, there were eighty-six family names listed for Cades Cove; by 1880, this had dropped to forty-five. Nevertheless, there was steady population growth through the latter part of the nineteenth century. By 1900, there were 708 residents in the cove—most of them related in one way or another.

Given the close kinship of cove residents, there was a generally egalitarian attitude. Status was determined more or less by one's behavior, not

Dan Lawson place, Cades Cove.

by one's birth or wealth. As a consequence, it is not surprising that there was a general sense of equality among all people, and mountain residents were openly sympathetic to the abolition of slavery. Still, during the Civil War, residents of the mountains were split in terms of their allegiances. Though southerners by geography, many residents of Cades Cove and other mountain communities were Union supporters. Part of the reason for their pro-Union attitudes was that few mountain people owned slaves. The 1850 and 1860 censuses listed no slaves in Cades Cove, although some surrounding communities did have slaveholders. Not surprisingly, in 1861, Blount County (which includes Cades Cove) voted 1,552 to 450 against secession from the Union.

East Tennessee residents threatened to secede from the Confederacy and join the Union. In response, Confederate troops were stationed in the region to keep it under rebel control. Guerrilla warfare against Union sympathizers occurred throughout the war. Fields were raided, and cattle, sheep, pigs, and horses were frequently stolen. Some residents were even murdered or simply disappeared. No one felt safe. Pro-Union cove men took to sleeping in the woods at night to avoid being taken prisoner or killed.

After the Civil War, the region went into severe decline. Though the soil was still relatively fertile, the opening of new lands in the West and declining market demand reduced the overall profitability of mountain farms. Furthermore, with new opportunities in the West, few new residents were migrating to the valley. The region more or less stood still or even regressed while the rest of the nation marched onward.

Alcohol production, or moonshine, was central to the mountain economy. Corn, grains, and fruits were all grown and used to produce whiskey and other products. Particularly when transportation networks were poor, turning corn or other grains into a high-value product such as whiskey was the only way for mountain residents to turn a profit on their crops. The greater the federal tax on alcoholic spirits, the greater the inducement for moonshining. Just as often, however, the moonshiner drank away any profits, and this often led to impoverishment of the family. Nevertheless, there appeared to be substantial local support for moonshining, and local and state officials often failed to prosecute individuals apprehended.

When national Prohibition was initiated in 1919, distilling liquor became very profitable. Compared with other parts of the South, the mountains that once isolated communities now provided a relative sanctuary from federal agents. Moonshining soon became a part-time or full-time occupation of mountain farmers. According to Horace Kephart in his book *Our Southern Highlanders*, once Prohibition became law, the profitability of moonshining went through the roof. Mountaineers were able to garner $10 to $20 a gallon and earn $1,000 or more in a few weeks. For impoverished mountain farmers, the economic incentive to brew a little moonshine was difficult to overlook.

The Logging Era

The timber industry had its origins in the northeastern United States. After cutting over the forests of Maine, New York, and Pennsylvania, the industry moved to the Midwest from Ohio to Minnesota, then leaped across the Rockies to the Pacific Coast states. Nevertheless, by 1900, the best forests with the most valuable trees lay in the South. Although the mountaineers who lived in the valleys surrounding the Smokies cut and used wood for many domestic purposes, large commercial timber operations moved into the area only after the turn of the century. From 1900 to 1920, the South led the nation in timber production. Even in

1901, most of the South's forests had experienced some commercial timber cutting.

A report on Appalachian forests prepared for the Department of Agriculture by foresters H. B. Ayers and W. W. Ashe reviewed 5.4 million acres from Virginia to Alabama and found that only 7.4 percent had never been visited by an ax or saw. Most of this native forest was in the steepest and most rugged terrain—places like the Smokies. Indeed, in the entire survey region, Ayers and Ashe reported that the Smokies and surrounding highlands had the largest continuous forest cover in all of Appalachia. According to their survey, less than 10 percent of the forest had ever been cleared. The Smokies contained the largest stands of spruce in the southern forests, plus some of the finest chestnut and other hardwood forests in the South.

Some of these hardwoods were immense, particularly the yellow poplar and chestnut trees. Kephart described some of these giants in *Our Southern Highlanders*. "On north fronts of hills the oaks reach a diameter of five to six feet. In cool, rich coves, chestnuts grow from six to nine feet across the stump; and tulip poplars up to ten or eleven feet, their straight trunks towering like gigantic columns, with scarcely a noticeable taper, seventy or eighty feet to the nearest limb." Such trees rivaled the giant Douglas firs and sugar pines of the Pacific Coast and, not surprisingly, caught the eye of the lumbermen.

Between 1896 and 1900, logs were cut and floated down the Little River to a mill in Lenoir City. River floats were used to log other stands of mountain forest. But it was the construction of logging railroads that led to big-time timber liquidation. Railroad construction was expensive, and paying for such an investment required scalping the mountains of most of their trees. Narrow-gauge rail lines were constructed up many river valleys, moving ever higher into the mountains. On the steepest terrain, oxen were used to drag the logs to landings, where they could be piled on railcars for the ride to the mill. Logging railroads were constructed up the Oconaluftee, Big Creek, Cataloochee, Big Pigeon, and Little River, among other sites now within GSMNP.

At the highest reaches, logs were skidded by horses. At times, splash dams would be built on small tributaries. Logs were stockpiled in the resulting ponds. Then, with sticks of dynamite, the dams would be blown up, and the rushing water would carry the logs far down the stream to a

Much of what is now GSMNP was purchased from timber companies. Despite the history of logging, enough of the land now part of the park was never logged and contains the largest tracts of old-growth timber left in the eastern United States.

river or mill below. Another transportation method was the flume, a narrow wooden aqueduct that carried logs downhill to a mill or river. Spruce from Clingmans Dome was once carried by a flume.

One of the first big-time lumber operations was started by Colonel W. B. Townsend, for whom Townsend, Tennessee, is named. Townsend moved from Pennsylvania and purchased 86,000 acres of land on the Little River that stretched from the summit of the Smokies to Tuckaleechee Cove. In 1901, Townsend chartered the Little River Company, constructed a mill in Townsend, and built a logging railroad up the Little River to access the timber on the slopes of the Smokies. Other large companies soon followed Townsend's example. The Ritter Lumber Company acquired land on Hazel Creek; Montvale Timber Company operated on Eagle Creek; Norwood Lumber worked over Forney Creek; Parsons Pulp and Lumber Company put a mill on the Raven Fork of the Oconaluftee River; and Champion purchased 92,000 acres in four large parcels, including lands in Greenbrier Cove, along Deep Creek, in the Oconaluftee drainage, and along the crest of the Smokies from Clingmans Dome to Mount Kephart. Champion built a sawmill at Smokemont and began to log the high-elevation spruce-fir forests along the Smokies' crest. By 1909, logging was at its peak. This intensified logging created a number of "mill towns" on the fringes of the Smokies, including Bryson City, Gatlinburg, Townsend, Elkmont, Ravensford, Proctor, and Fontana. Today, tourism has long surpassed logging as the main economic enterprise in most of these communities, or, as in the case of Elkmont, they have been completely abandoned.

Though the timber companies made a fortune, the loggers in this era—prior to unions and worker safety—were paid poorly for extremely dangerous work. The typical logger received a mere dollar a day for his efforts, plus room and board in remote logging camps. The days were long, and the work brutal. Accidents were frequent. But labor, like the trees, were expendable.

Despite the hazardous nature of the work, many of the small farmers of the Smokies welcomed these logging companies into the mountains. Even the poor pay was better than no pay. With few other employment opportunities, logging jobs helped put cash in the pockets of the region's farm families. The logging camps were also a reliable market for produce from the farms, including fresh vegetables, meat, and dairy products.

By the 1920s, an estimated two-thirds of the Smokies had been logged over or burned by fires caused by logging operations. People were beginning to question whether more logging of the virgin forests was really the best use of these lands. Horace Kephart, an early park supporter, described his feelings when he visited a recently logged site: "When I first came to the Smokies the whole region was one superb forest primeval. I lived for several years in the heart of it. My sylvan studio spread over mountain after mountain, seemingly without end, and it was always clean and fragrant, always vital, growing new shapes of beauty from day to day. The vast trees met overhead like cathedral roofs. . . . Not long ago I went to that same place again. It was wrecked, ruined, desecrated, turned into a thousand rubbish heaps, utterly vile and mean."

Nevertheless, pockets of virgin timber remained, particularly in the highest, steepest drainages. It was recognition that the Smokies offered the best opportunities for protecting and preserving tracts of virgin forest that ultimately led to its nomination as a potential national park.

The Park Idea

Although the push for a park took on new urgency when logging began to ravage the forests, the idea for establishing a national park in the Smokies had been on people's minds for some time. The concept had begun to take hold before the turn of the twentieth century. The nation's first national park, Yellowstone, was created in 1872. Both Yosemite and Sequoia National Parks were established in 1890. These events prompted people in other parts of the country to think about their scenic wonders that might be suitable for national park status. Not surprisingly, some residents of the Southeast looked at the southern Appalachians as potential national park material. As early as the 1880s, state geologist Drayton Smith of Franklin, North Carolina, proposed a national park in the mountains of western North Carolina. In 1885, Dr. Henry Marcy of Boston suggested putting aside a tract of land under "state control . . . in the higher range as a park." In 1893, the North Carolina general assembly passed a resolution urging Congress to create a national park in the region. Although the idea was presented to Congress by Representative John Henderson of North Carolina, no further action occurred. In 1899, a park advocacy group was established in Asheville, North Carolina, to promote the concept of a national park someplace in the southern Appalachian region.

Creating a national park in the eastern United States involved some unique problems that were not faced by western park advocates. Unlike in the West, where much of the land was under federal control and thus already owned by the public, nearly all the land in the East had passed into private ownership in colonial times or soon afterward. Any new park in the East would have to be acquired through fee purchase.

In addition to the problem of paying for the land, parks were in competition with other land-use plans that were taking hold. The creation of national parks was part of a growing conservation movement, and other public lands were being set aside as national forests. The first national forest was created in 1891 when the Yellowstone Timber Reserve was designated immediately adjacent to Yellowstone National Park, and other national forests were designated throughout the West. National forests differed from national parks in that they typically permitted some regulated activities such as logging, mining, and grazing that were prohibited in national parks. Thus, many who opposed national parks as too restrictive often supported the creation of national forests. As more national parks were carved from the public domain, national forests became an attractive alternative, sometimes successfully sapping support for parks.

The national forest movement was spearheaded by Gifford Pinchot, who gained fame and influence after he developed a forestry plan for George Vanderbilt's Biltmore estate near Asheville. Pinchot later became the first director of the U.S. Forest Service and governor of Pennsylvania. He was a staunch advocate of public ownership of natural resources such as forests. Such a concept was—at the time—nearly foreign to the frontier mentality, which was dominated by natural resource exploitation. Pinchot tempered his call for government supervision by supporting controlled logging, grazing, and other activities. He lobbied to set up the U.S. Forest Service and helped establish many new national forests on federal lands in the western United States. Pinchot saw a need for national forests in the East as well, but creating such forests would require both special legislation and federal funding.

In 1901, Senator Pritchard of North Carolina introduced two bills in Congress. One funded the study of the status of southern Appalachian forests eventually completed by Ayers and Ashe. A second bill authorized $5 million to acquire lands for forest reserves in the southern Appalachian Mountains. The land acquisitions were held up for years by congressional politics, but the forestry study was completed in 1901 and endorsed by President Theodore Roosevelt. Roosevelt wrote enthusiastically about the need to protect southern Appalachian forestlands:

> In this region occur that marvelous variety and richness of plant growth which have led our ablest businessmen and scientists to ask for its preservation by the Government for the advancement of science and for the instruction and pleasure of the people of our own and of future generations. And it is the concentration here of so many valuable species with such favorable conditions of growth which has led forest experts and lumbermen alike to assert that of all the continent this region is best suited to the purposes and plans of a national forest reserve in the hardwood region.

Despite Roosevelt's strong support, lumber interests and their allies in Congress managed to stop all legislation calling for the establishment of new national forests in the region. It was not until 1911 that the Weeks Act passed, permitting the creation of national forests in the East through the acquisition of private lands. Under the act, each potential new national forest would have a purchase area boundary established, within which the federal government would seek to acquire all lands. Almost immediately, the Great Smoky Mountains region was targeted as such a purchase area. Between 1911 and 1916, the federal government acquired an option to purchase some 61,350 acres from the Little River Lumber Company for the creation of a new national forest in the Smokies. But shaky land titles, combined with higher lumber prices created by the onset of World War I, caused the deal to fall through, and the movement to create a national forest in the Smokies failed.

At the time the Weeks Act passed, there were already dozens of national parks and monuments in the western United States, including Yellowstone, Sequoia, Yosemite, and Glacier National Parks. Nevertheless, there was no centralized federal agency directly responsible for their operation. Congress established the National Park Service in 1916 to oversee the park system. In a 1923 annual report, the agency's director, Stephen Mather, called for the creation of a national park in the Appalachian Range.

Several bills authorizing a national park in various locations in the Appalachians were introduced in Congress in 1922 and 1923. Nothing came of them, but clearly, momentum was building for some kind of protected landscape in the southern Appalachians.

Horses by Sparks Lane, Cades Cove. In the 1920s, a movement to create a national park someplace in the southern Appalachians led to a review of numerous sites from the Shenendoah Valley to the Smokies, including Roan Mountain, Grandfather Mountain, and Cumberland Gap. After visiting all the sites, the committee selected the Great Smoky Mountains "because of the height of the mountains, depth of valleys, ruggedness of the area, and the unexampled variety of tree, shrubs, and plants."

In 1924, Secretary of the Interior Hubert Work appointed a five-person committee to study the Appalachians and recommend a site for an eastern national park. The committee initially was leaning toward the Shenandoah region of Virginia, but in response to protests from residents of other regions who were advocates of their own backyards, the park committee organized a tour of the entire southern Appalachian region that summer. A number of sites in North Carolina were under consideration, including Roan Mountain, Mount Mitchell, Grandfather Mountain, and Linville

Gorge. The park committee arrived in Asheville for its visit to these locations, when a delegation from Knoxville, Tennessee, showed up to urge the committee to visit the Smokies as a potential park site. Persistent efforts by the Tennessee delegation finally convinced two committee members to inspect the area. Traveling on horseback, they spent six days in the Mount LeConte region with twenty-five Tennessee Smoky Mountains advocates.

Throughout the summer and fall, committee members visited other sites in the region. In December 1924, they met to make their choice. The committee report noted:

> We inspected the northern part of Georgia, whose fine mountains blend with the Highland region of southern North Carolina. We ascended Mount Mitchell and viewed the splendid Black Mountain Range north of Asheville. We went over carefully the Grandfather Mountain region, which for our study included the beautiful country from Blowing Rock to the remarkable Linville Gorge. We responded to the call of the poet—to see Roan Mountain if we could really see the southern Appalachians. We went to Knoxville and from there to the tops of the "Big Smokies" which carry on their crest the boundary line between North Carolina and Tennessee. We went into Virginia to inspect that portion of the Blue Ridge on the east side of the Shenandoah Valley which extends from Front Royal to Waynesboro. Some members of the committee also visited Cumberland Gap, southern West Virginia, northern Alabama, and eastern Kentucky. Several areas were found that contained topographic features of great scenic value, where waterfalls, cascades, cliffs, and mountain peaks, with beautiful valleys lying in their midst, gave ample assurance that any or all of these areas were possible for development into a national park which would compare favorably with any of the existing national parks in the West.

After deliberation of all these sites—which the committee suggested were all worthy of being parks—the committee concluded that the Great Smoky Mountains easily stood first among park candidates "because of the height of the mountains, depth of valleys, ruggedness of the area, and the unexampled variety of tree, shrubs, and plants." But the committee had some concerns about the Smokies as well. For example, their ruggedness would hinder the development of roads and thus limit access to visitors. So, the committee determined that the Blue Ridge of Virginia was the logical place for a new national park in the southern Appalachians. However, it urged the secretary of the interior to create a second park in the Great Smoky Mountains.

In 1925, a bill was introduced in both houses of Congress authorizing national parks in the region—Smoky Mountains, Shenandoah, and Mammoth Cave. Although the parks were authorized, Congress did not appropriate funds to purchase land for these parks. The government, however, could accept land and money for them. In effect, Congress acknowledged that creation of national parks in the southern Appalachian region was desirable, but it was not going to make it happen. If parks were going to be more than a dream, citizen support would be required.

The Push for a Park

Fortunately, it didn't take long for people in the region to respond. Later in the year, the state of Tennessee negotiated a deal with the Little River Lumber Company to purchase 76,507 acres of land in the Smokies. Opposition to the plan was intense, and the state legislature failed to support the funding request. In response, park champions in Knoxville chartered a train to take members of the legislature to see the Smokies firsthand. In addition, Knoxville agreed to pay one-third of the purchase price, if necessary, to encourage the state to buy the timber holdings. With this as a strong endorsement, the legislature was persuaded to support the land purchase and eventually funded the deal, taking the first major step toward realization of a park in the Smoky Mountains.

The major motivation behind the creation of a national park in the Smokies—at least from the perspective of the city of Knoxville and the state of Tennessee—was not so much altruistic as financial. People thought that a national park would be a big economic engine that would create jobs in the region. Even the National Park Service promoted parks in part based on the financial opportunities they would create for communities and states. Certainly there is plenty of evidence throughout the country that national parks are exactly that—big moneymakers for the regional economies. Besides creating jobs in the tourism industry, protected landscapes are seen as desirable places to live, attracting new residents and businesses that have no direct stake in tourism. Still, in many instances, the motivations of the most dedicated and ardent park proponents go well beyond financial concerns. Most national park advocates are concerned with protecting natural landscapes for future generations and the general ecological health of the area. This was certainly the case for the promoters of GSMNP.

If it were not for some prominent and steadfast support from a handful of Knoxville residents, GSMNP may never have overcome all the hurdles placed in the path of the park's establishment. Among the more vocal Knoxville supporters were Mr. and Mrs. Willis Davis and David Chapman. Together they formed the Great Smoky Mountains Conservation Association. Although they certainly touted the economic advantages of a national park, their prime motivation seems to have been a desire to protect the beauty and wildlands of the Great Smoky Mountains.

In contrast to the support for a park by Tennessee and especially Knoxville, opposition to a park in the Smokies was more intense on the North Carolina side of the mountains. In particular, timber companies were opposed to any park in the area, and most were unwilling to sell their land for a park. But North Carolina had its park supporters as well. One of the most ardent and eloquent was author Horace Kephart, who had moved to the region in 1904 at age forty-two to find rejuvenation in the mountains. He spent years exploring, camping, fishing, and gaining back his health and stamina. After settling in Bryson City, Kephart wrote several well-received books, including *Camping and Woodcraft* and *Our Southern Highlanders*. He also penned numerous letters to the local papers in support of a national park in the Smokies. Since many park opponents were advocates of national forest designation for the Smokies, Kephart also wrote frequently about his opposition to that alternative: "Why should this last stand of splendid, irreplaceable trees be sacrificed to the greedy maw of the sawmill? Why should future generations be robbed of all chance to see with their own eyes what a real forest, a real wildwood, a real unimproved work of God is like."

Even today, opponents of forest protection usually try to argue that there is a great national need to exploit the resources found in the last pockets of wildlands and that somehow the nation will suffer if the last tree is not cut into a two-by-four. Such arguments were rampant in North Carolina in Kephart's day as well, and he responded by arguing: "It is all nonsense to say that the country needs the timber. If every stick of it were cut, the output would be a mere drop in the bucket compared to the annual production of lumber in America. Let these few old trees stand! Let the nation save them inviolate by treating them as national monuments in a national park."

Even if the idea of a park were supported by the surrounding states, purchasing the property to create the park involved enormous obstacles. Most of the larger tracts of land were owned by timber companies, which controlled 85 percent of the land within the proposed park. Many of them were openly hostile to the park idea and unwilling to sell their land. There were many small-tract property holders as well, including 1,200 farmers and 5,000 small-lot and summer-home owners. In total, more than 6,000 individuals and companies controlled the property within the proposed park. Each one had to be contacted individually and had to agree to sell its land for the park.

Even without opposition from timber interests and others, the fund-raising obstacles were immense. Yet public support continued to grow. In Knoxville and surrounding communities, schoolchildren donated pennies to support the park acquisitions. Individuals such as David Chapman contributed thousands of dollars. The Asheville Chamber of Commerce contributed $25,000. By 1926, more than $1 million in citizen contributions had been raised in Tennessee and North Carolina, and those two states contributed another $4 million. Still, this was not enough to complete the park purchases. Philanthropist John D. Rockefeller came to the rescue. The $5 million raised by citizens and state legislatures was matched by a grant from Rockefeller and from the Laura Spelman Rockefeller Memorial Fund. With $10 million in the pot, park advocates began to contact potential sellers about land acquisitions.

The first parcel bought for the park was the Little River Lumber Company property. But Colonel Townsend, who owned the land, would agree to the sale only if his company could continue to cut timber for fifteen years. As the acquisition process continued, many other timber companies were defiantly cutting trees, hoping that by destroying the forest, they would destroy the desire for a park there. A showdown was inevitable. The North Carolina Park Commission sought to purchase 26,000 acres from the Sunset Lumber Company, but the company refused to accept the appraised value and continued to cut trees. Finally, the Park Commission brought a suit against Sunset Lumber to force it to halt its logging. The circuit court of appeals ruled in favor of the Park Commission, but the company took the case all the way to the U.S. Supreme Court. A similar case against the Ravensford Lumber Company over 32,700 acres it held within the proposed park also went to the Supreme Court. In both cases, the Court ordered the companies to halt logging the forests and sell their land for the park.

As difficult as these purchases were, opposition from Champion Fiber Company had the greatest potential to torpedo the park proposal. Champion owned 90,000 acres in the heart of the park area, including Mount LeConte, Newfound Gap, Clingmans Dome, and Mount Guyot. Without this land, the park could not be completed. In 1930, the Tennessee Park Commission went to court to obtain eminent domain condemnation against the company. Through negotiations, the company finally accepted an offer of $3 million for its holdings.

We can be thankful that the use of eminent domain to condemn and purchase land for parks was well supported by the government and the courts back then. It is difficult to imagine that such tactics would be successful today, even though we have an even greater understanding of the need to protect natural landscapes.

Though difficult and often done without cooperation from the timber companies, buying land from them had a benefit as well—in one sale, tens of thousands of acres could be acquired, often for a reasonable price per acre. For instance, the Little River Lumber Company sold 75,000 acres in the park area for $3.57 an acre. Other companies were less willing to negotiate but eventually sold their holdings.

Despite the land acquisition problems in North Carolina, in many ways, buying land for the park was far more difficult on the Tennessee side of the border. Instead of dealing with just a few large landowning corporations, park advocates had to buy land from thousands of small landholders, many of whom had emotional attachments to the land. Reaction to the park concept varied tremendously among the farmers and other landowners in the mountains. Some, particularly the poor mountain farmers, were glad to sell out and begin a new life elsewhere. But others staunchly opposed the creation of the park, including John W. Oliver, a descendant of the original homesteader of Cades Cove. Condemnation proceedings were filed against Oliver in 1929. He fought the process for years, going before the Tennessee Supreme Court three times before he reluctantly agreed to sell his property.

Funds were getting scarce by then, and it took additional expenditures from the federal government to complete the land purchases for the park. President Franklin D. Roosevelt came to the rescue with an executive

Mill Creek, Cades Cove. Since all of the land that is now within GSMNP was originally in private hands, the entire park had to be bought acre by acre, parcel by parcel. Most of the larger tracts were purchased from timber companies, but more than 5,000 small tracts were also bought to complete the park acquisitions.

order authorizing $1.5 million in federal funds to complete land purchases in the Smokies. The Rockefeller Memorial then made an additional contribution. Altogether, more than $12 million was spent on land for the proposed park—an investment that has reaped billions in tourism-related jobs and income since then, not to mention uncounted biological value.

By 1935, more than 400,000 acres were in public ownership, and the Great Smoky Mountains qualified for full national park status, as required by the original legislation. But more lands were sought, and in 1938, Congress finally appropriated $743,265 for land acquisition. In total, the states of Tennessee and North Carolina contributed $4,095,696 for land acquisition; the U.S. government gave another $3,503,766; and the Rockefeller Memorial contributed the greatest amount, totaling $5,065,000. Without the philanthropy of John D. Rockefeller, whose strategic contributions helped acquire key parcels, there might not be a GSMNP today.

In 1940, President Franklin D. Roosevelt dedicated the park.

Changes in the Park

The new park brought about changes in the mountains. Some of the old farms and timberlands were permitted to regrow into forest. There are numerous old fields throughout the park that are now forested. At the same time, new developments, including roads and campgrounds, were improved or created to make the park more accessible to visitors. For instance, Newfound Gap Road was upgraded and paved, providing a cross-park roadway that also provides a spur to Clingmans Dome near the crest of the range.

Construction of the Foothills Parkway began in 1960. Although the entire 71-mile roadway is outside of the park, the Park Service administers the road. Another road through the heart of the park was proposed in 1965. The road would have connected Fontana Lake via a road up Eagle Creek, over Buckeye Gap, and down to Townsend Y. Fortunately for the park wildlands, opposition was so strong that the secretary of the interior abandoned plans for the road.

A new road may soon be built along the southeast perimeter of the park near Fontana Reservoir. The road is part of a long-standing controversy. When the Tennessee Valley Authority constructed Fontana Dam, it cut off part of Swain County and flooded Highway 288. To compensate for the loss of land, the TVA purchased 44,170 acres that were added to the park. In exchange, the Park Service was instructed to build a road along the north shore of the reservoir. However, with changing views about development and its role in preserving intact ecosystems, the Park Service shifted its priorities toward greater protection of the land, and the road was never built. For years, residents of the region have lobbied for a new road. Opposition to the road from wilderness advocates has been intense. For one thing, the road would cut through the edge of the largest remaining roadless section of the park and allow increased visitation to what is now the most remote part of the park. It would also offer a new route for exotic plants and animals to invade the park and contribute to greater habitat fragmentation.

The issue of road construction has thwarted environmentalists, who support permanent protection of the park's roadless backcountry through its designation as wilderness under the 1964 Wilderness Act. If the park were added to the national wilderness system, future road building would be prohibited. The Smokies constitute one of the largest tracts of wild-lands in the eastern United States, and certainly much of the park qualifies as wilderness under the terms of the Wilderness Act. Opposition from some North Carolina politicians has held up the designation of any park lands under the Wilderness Act. The Park Service currently manages the park as de facto wilderness, but it seems that those intent on increasing development and destruction of the park's natural features have thus far held the wilderness question hostage.

The Future

The greatest value of GSMNP lies in the future. As the largest tract of intact virgin forest in the eastern United States, and situated in the midst of another 2.5 million acres of national forest lands, GSMNP is the core of the largest wildlands complex in the Southeast. Protecting the native flora and fauna and the ecological processes that support them is now recognized as one of the greatest challenges facing park managers. Controlling exotic species such as wild hogs and restoring native species such as brook trout are two obvious ways that the Park Service is rising to the challenge. Yet GSMNP does not exist as an island. Often the management of adjacent lands is at odds with preserving the ecological integrity of what is undisputedly one of the most biologically rich areas in the entire United States.

The surrounding public and private lands, particularly those under Forest Service administration, should complement the ecological protection goals of the Park Service. Wilderness designation for all roadless Forest Service lands could be the first step in protecting this region. Less than 10 percent of the six national forests in the southern Appalachian region is protected as congressionally designated wilderness. Wilderness could become the core of a larger system of wildlands and buffers managed to preserve the ecological integrity of the region.

But designation of wilderness is not enough. We need to restore many lands, preserve connecting corridors, and, in some cases, remove or terminate those elements that are threatening the region—whether they be air pollution killing spruce-fir forests, or private land development that fragments the forests. To protect this internationally important region, creation of a Greater Smoky Mountains Ecosystem is needed, with GSMNP as the core. The goal would be to manage the entire region as one ecological whole. Management or development that does not contribute to the preservation of the region's ecological integrity should be phased out or eliminated. Acquisition of biologically important private lands should become a high priority of land trusts and government agencies. Creation of a Greater Smoky Mountains Ecosystem could be a rallying point and could create a new way of thinking about the region.

GEOLOGY

The mountains of GSMNP are part of the Appalachian chain that stretches from Newfoundland to Alabama. The southern part of the chain from Pennsylvania to Georgia has four major parallel subdivisions: the Piedmont, Blue Ridge, Ridge and Valley, and Appalachian Plateaus. The oldest rocks are in the east along the Piedmont, with the rock formations becoming progressively younger as one moves west to the Appalachian Plateau. The southern Appalachian Mountains are many miles wide and encompass numerous separately named subranges, including the Great Smoky Mountains, the Black Range, the Nantahala Mountains, the Balsams, and other highlands. The highest peak in the Appalachian chain is 6,684-foot Mount Mitchell in the Black Range. These individually named ranges often reflect their slightly different geological origins. Yet across the entire chain of mountains, there are common geological processes that have contributed to their appearance and features.

Before discussing the geological origins of the southern Appalachian Mountains, it is necessary to become familiar with some basic terms and concepts, such as geological time, rock types, and tectonic theory.

Geological Time

The earth is thought to be at least 4.5 billion years old. There are few records from the early years of earth history, because the vast majority of geological history was destroyed by subsequent geological events, including the movement of continents and erosion. The earliest era, and by far the longest, is known as the Precambrian. It spans the period from the planet's birth to 570 million years ago. The majority of the rocks found in GSMNP were formed during the late Precambrian era, making them quite old compared with rocks in other parts of the United States.

After the Precambrian era came the Paleozoic, which lasted from 570 million to 230 million years ago. During this era, early forms of life began to flourish on earth, including shellfish, fish, and amphibians. Only 10 percent of the rocks in GSMNP are from the Paleozoic era, and they are found on the western edge of the park in Cades Cove and on Chilhowee Mountain, among other locations.

The next era is the Mesozoic, which lasted from 230 million to 65 million years ago. This was the age of the reptiles, best known for the dinosaurs that flourished during this period. No rocks of this age are found in the park.

The final major era is the Cenozoic, which includes everything from the demise of dinosaurs some 65 million years ago to the present. This is the time when mammals came to dominate the earth. There are no major outcrops of rocks in GSMNP from this era either.

Rock Types

There are three major types of rocks: sedimentary, igneous, and metamorphic. Sedimentary rocks are typically formed in ocean basins when river sediments washed into the sea or the remains of sea life are deposited in horizontal layers and later cemented into stone. Typical examples of sedimentary rock are sandstone, limestone, and mudstone. Sedimentary rocks are abundant in the park.

Igneous rock is created from molten magma that later cools deep in the earth or is deposited on the surface as lava. Two common forms of igneous rock are granite and basalt. Igneous rocks are rare in GSMNP.

Metamorphic rock can be derived from either sedimentary or igneous rock. Under conditions of heat and pressure, either type of rock can be changed, or metamorphosed, into another kind of rock. For instance, limestone can be changed into marble. Generally, the older the rock material, the more likely it is to be changed. Not surprisingly, given the ancient origins of many of the rocks in GSMNP, metamorphic rocks are common in the park.

Tectonic Theory

Tectonic theory helps explain the earth's present landscape features and rock structure. It holds that the earth's surface is made up of a dozen or so large plates and many smaller fragments that float on a semiliquid mantle. Radioactive decay in the mantle creates heat, which produces convection currents that slowly move the floating continental plates across the surface of the earth. Some plates break apart, others collide, and some override others. For instance, today's Atlantic Ocean basin was created by a rift along a north-south seam in its middle. Molten lava came to the surface of the ocean floor to create a new sea bottom, while the plates that Europe and North America ride on moved farther away from each other. The Himalaya Mountains lie along a collision zone where the Indian subcontinent piled up against Asia, thrusting up the highest mountains on earth in the process. This continual movement of plates mixes up rocks from many different sources to create a hodgepodge of rocks that form the present-day continents.

Like the Himalayas, the Appalachian Mountains were also created by a collision of continents. Rock strata were crushed, bent, broken, folded, and shoved past one another. Some of the original sedimentary rocks in GSMNP were metamorphosed by this process, changing them into slate, quartzite, and other meta-sedimentary rocks. Erosion worked on all these rocks, removing the softer shale, slate, and limestone and leaving the more durable sandstone, siltstone, and quartzite behind.

Geological History of GSMNP

The majority of rocks in GSMNP were formed during the Precambrian era. For most of this period, there was no life on earth. The oldest of these rocks are basement rocks that were originally either marine sedimentary rocks or igneous rocks. Many of these rocks were later crunched, compressed, and changed by heat into metamorphic rocks, which were later exposed by erosion.

In the late Precambrian era, new sediments accumulated on a broad continental shelf. These rocks, known as the Ocoee Supergroup, were primarily sandstone, slate, siltstone, and shale. Most of these rocks were subsequently changed to some degree by future geological events.

Some 500 to 600 million years ago, near the end of the Precambrian era and the beginning of the Paleozoic, the Western and Eastern Hemispheres collided, forming a large land mass known as Gondwana. Rocks along the margins of this collision point were folded and compressed and, in some instances, slid over and above others.

By 300 million years ago, North America was near the equator, and the climate was warm and humid. Large amounts of carboniferous materials were deposited in shallow seas; these later became the vast coalfields of Kentucky and West Virginia, along the margins of today's mountains. By

290 million years ago, the collision of continents was complete, and all the continents except China were united into a supercontinent known as Pangea. The collision caused the Appalachians to rise to great heights, blocking the movement of air masses and creating a desert in the rain shadow of the mountains, much as today's Sierra Nevadas in California have created a desert to the east in Death Valley. With the drier climate, the coal-forming forests began to disappear. By 240 million years ago, the drying conditions favored the development and rise of reptiles. With lungs; tough, watertight skin; and the ability to lay eggs on land rather than in the water like frogs and other amphibians, reptiles could survive in arid lands.

Pangea began to break apart about 205 million years ago, around the time that the dinosaurs were beginning to populate the earth. North America slowly began to split from Europe and North Africa, and the Atlantic Ocean was born. Evidence of this rupture can be found among the rocks: rocks with origins in the plates that make up Europe and Africa are also part of the North American continent—for instance, the rock beneath Boston may have been part of Africa at one time. After the split, North America drifted west and northward into its present configuration.

The collision of continents placed great stress on the rocks in the region, creating numerous faults. This faulting process created a major geological enigma: Most of the ancient rocks that are visible at the surface of the Great Smoky Mountains are lying on top of younger rock strata, which is the opposite of what one would expect. The oldest rocks should be at the bottom of the pile, since presumably they were laid down first. But in GSMNP, this isn't the case.

There are four major faults in the park—Great Smoky, Gatlinburg, Greenbrier, and Oconaluftee. The Great Smoky Fault, the most westerly, has moved thousands of feet, pushing Precambrian bedrock up and over younger Paleozoic rocks of eastern Tennessee. In some places, erosion has worn through this overlying Precambrian bedrock to create a "window" that exposes the younger Paleozoic rock beneath. Today, we call these mountain-rimmed valleys *coves*. Cades Cove in GSMNP and Tuckalee-chee and Wears Coves just outside the park are examples of these erosion-created windows. These coves are dominated by Paleozoic limestone. Water percolating through these predominately limestone areas of the park created a number of karst features, including Bull Cave, Gregory Cave, Blowing Cave, and Rainbow Cave.

Cades Cove is a "window" in the bedrock. The mountain-rimmed valley was created when rocks originally found in North Carolina were shoved thousands of feet westward by the Great Smoky Fault. This movement pushed Precambrian bedrock up and over younger Paleozoic rocks of eastern Tennessee. In some places like Cades Cove, erosion has worn through this overlying Precambrian bedrock to create a "window" that exposes the younger Paleozoic rock beneath. Today, we call these mountain-rimmed valleys coves. Cades Cove in GSMNP and Tuckaleechee and Wears Coves just outside the park are examples of these erosion-created windows. These coves are dominated by Paleozoic limestones that form productive soils.

The underlying bedrock in the park consists of the three major types: sedimentary, igneous, and metamorphic. In the southeastern and southern parts of GSMNP are billion-year-old crystalline Precambrian basement rocks. These consist of both metamorphic and igneous rocks such as schist, gneiss, and granitic rocks that were formed under heat and pressure into relatively erosion-resistant bedrock. Outcrops can be seen near Bryson City, Cherokee, Maggie Valley, Deep Creek Campground, and Oconaluftee visitor center and along the Raven Fork. The same rocks make up the bulk of the Blue Ridge Mountains north and east of GSMNP.

The dominant rock type found in GSMNP, making up the majority of the park's mountains, is metamorphosed sedimentary rock. Most of these rocks are 500 million to 1 billion years old—well before there were dinosaurs or even fish. The most common rocks of this type are the Ocoee Supergroup, which is subdivided into three main groups: Walden Creek, Great Smoky, and Snowbird. Finally, each group is further divided by thirteen formations, with the Thunderhead and Anakeesta Formations the most common rocks in the park. These rocks extend well beyond GSMNP, spanning a distance of 175 miles from Asheville, North Carolina, in the north to Carterville, Georgia, in the south. They are part of a suspect terrane—a segment of crust of unknown origin that was attached to the North American continent sometime in the distant past. Along

Looking east toward North Carolina from Newfound Gap. Most of the rocks seen along the Newfound Gap Road consist of the Ocoee Supergroup metamorphosed sedimentary sequences. Outcrops of these rocks make up such prominent park features as Clingmans Dome, Mount LeConte, and the Chimney Tops.

the northwest edge of GSMNP these rocks have been thrust over the younger Paleozoic rocks of the Appalachian Valley to the west.

Sedimentary rocks are the youngest rocks found in the park, ranging from 300 to 500 million years in age. Included are the shale, sandstone, and limestone that can be seen at Whiteoak Sink and Cades Cove and along the Foothills Parkway.

Present-Day Geomorphological Processes

The mountains we see today are partially the result of uplift along faults, as well as erosion. Water is the primary erosion agent, although freeze-thaw processes also contributed to the present-day landscape. With the heavy rainfall that cascades down these mountains, there is plenty of opportunity for water to participate in the mountain-sculpting processes.

As the mountains were uplifted, the gradient of streams increased, giving them greater power to erode and carry away sediments. Most of the streams in GSMNP follow weaknesses in the rock structure created by faulting. In other words, the grinding and crumpling of rock along fault lines created zones of weakened rock that water can exploit. Not

Water is the primary erosive agent in the park. Water-rounded stones lie among the bedrock exposed here along the Middle Prong of the Little Pigeon River.

surprisingly, the deep ravines common in the park are a consequence of both faulting and water erosion.

Water also helps wedge rock apart. It enters seams and cracks in the rock and, during winter, freezes and breaks the rock apart, exposing new surfaces to additional erosion. South-facing slopes experience greater temperature variation in winter and have a more rapid breakdown of rock as a consequence of the continual freezing and melting of water.

Water can also contribute to the breakdown of rock in another way. Some rocks, such as limestone, are easily dissolved by acid rainwater. The caves and sinkholes found in Cades Cove and other limestone outcrops are good examples of this process.

One obvious consequence of water erosion in GSMNP are the narrow, steep river valleys. In parts of the country where glaciation occurred, such valleys tend to be broader and more U-shaped. Water-cut valleys, such as those in GSMNP, are V-shaped.

Where to See Geological Exposures

The geology of GSMNP is not easily viewed because the heavy forest cover obscures all but the grossest features, such as river valleys and mountain peaks. Nevertheless, there are occasional road cuts, stream channels, and other places where some of the park's geological structure can be observed.

Almost everyone visiting GSMNP drives the Newfound Gap Road between Cherokee, North Carolina, and the park visitor center at Sugarlands. This road not only offers many scenic vistas but also provides an opportunity to see some of the park's major geological features. Most of the rocks seen along the Newfound Gap Road consist of the Ocoee Supergroup metamorphosed sedimentary sequences. Outcrops of these rocks make up such prominent park features as Clingmans Dome, Mount LeConte, and the Chimney Tops.

Beginning at Sugarlands, the dominant visible rock type is known as Roaring Fork Sandstone. Sandstone is sedimentary rock formed on the bottom of ocean basins. Just a few miles east of the visitor center, you cross the Greenbrier Fault, a major structural fault that outcrops again near the Oconaluftee ranger station on the other side of the mountains.

Just 2 miles from Sugarlands, you cross Elkmont Sandstone, another member of the Ocoee Supergroup. Less than 3 miles from Sugarlands is the Thunderhead Formation, another region of gray sandstone. The

Ramsay Cascades is formed when the Ramsay Prong flows over a resistant layer of Thunderhead Sandstone.

bedding, or layering, of the original sedimentary formations is obvious in some road cuts. You can also see how these layers were tilted slightly off of horizontal by the mountain-building forces. The erosion-resistant Thunderhead Sandstone is responsible for most of the waterfalls in the park.

After passing the parking area for the Chimney Tops trailhead, and about 8 miles from the visitor center, you cross on to the Anakeesta

Formation. These rocks account for most of the stone seen all the way to Newfound Gap, at more than 5,000 feet elevation. The Anakeesta Formation is slate and meta-siltstone formed from mud sediments. The rocks of this formation are rusty in color from oxidation of the mineral pyrite, or fool's gold.

Just after passing over Newfound Gap, you begin to descend into the Oconaluftee drainage and almost immediately cross the Oconaluftee Fault. The fault isn't visible, but the weakness in the rock created by the fault contributed to the formation of the valley.

As you descend the other side of the mountain, you again reenter a section of Thunderhead Sandstone.

Just 1.5 miles beyond the Smokemont Campground, you cross the Greenbrier Fault again. Like the Oconaluftee Fault, this fault is not visible, but a subtle change in rocks is noticeable just beyond the fault line. Some 2.5 miles past the Smokemont Campground, outcrops of the old Precambrian basement bedrock can occasionally be seen. This dark

The Chimneys along the Newfound Gap Road consists of an outcrop of shale that makes up the Anakeesta Formation.

gray granite-gneiss rock has numerous veins and masses of white quartz embedded in it. Unlike in sandstone, there is no obvious bedding or layering.

The next most popular road in the park is the Little River Road from the Sugarlands visitor center to Cades Cove. This is a good place to observe the underlying Paleozoic limestone exposed by erosion.

Starting from Sugarlands, the road passes through various meta-sedimentary rocks, including Roaring Fork Sandstone. About 4 miles

The Sinks Waterfall on the Little River pours over a titled layer of the Thunderhead Sandstone Formation.

from the visitor center, you cross Fighting Gap and pass the trail to Laurel Falls. This popular trail crosses beds of Thunderhead Sandstone, and the falls themselves were created by a resistance layer of the same rock formation.

By Elkmont, you encounter Elkmont Sandstone. Just beyond Elkmont, the road follows the Little River and again crosses Thunderhead Sandstone. The waterfall by the Sinks on the Little River was created by a resistance layer of Thunderhead Sandstone.

From the Sinks on to Cades Cove, the road crosses and recrosses the Greenbrier Fault several times. The fault is not visible, but the underlying rock changes with each crossing of the fault zone. Most of the way to Cades Cove, the road passes over Thunderhead Sandstone, Metcalf Phyllite Formation, and Cades Sandstone. Some 18.75 miles from Sugarlands, you enter the Laurel Creek Road tunnel. The rocks surrounding the tunnel entrance are the thin-layered shale known as Metcalf phyllite.

Upon entering Cades Cove on its one-way loop road, notice the lush vegetation, indicating the productive soils created by weathering of the underlying limestone. The Cades Cove Road crosses the Great Smoky Fault several times, but the fault itself is not visible. Hiking the popular trail to Abrams Falls located at the far western end of the loop road takes you back into Cades Sandstone. The falls was created by this erosion-resistant sandstone.

PLANTS

The hallmark of Great Smoky Mountains National Park is the tremendous diversity of its plant and animal life. This diversity is perhaps best expressed in the park's great variety of tree species—silverbells, yellow poplars, oaks, maples, birches, and magnolias, among others. Some botanists believe that there may be as many as 135 species of trees in the park's half-million acres. By comparison, in the entire state of Alaska—encompassing 375 million acres—there are only 33 native trees. The number of flowers, shrubs, and ferns in GSMNP easily exceeds another 1,500 species.

Such astounding diversity is a consequence of several factors: mild climate and abundant precipitation, great elevational change, and topographic diversity. This, combined with the past and present history of human use and influence, has made GSMNP a center for biodiversity.

The climate of GSMNP is relatively mild, humid, and well watered—ideal growing conditions for the many broadleaf species that dominate the park landscape. And unlike Alaska and even New England, the southern Appalachians were never overrun by glaciers. Indeed, the region was a refugium for many species that were extirpated from more northern latitudes by advancing ice sheets. Thus, species have had a much longer time to evolve and adapt to the local terrain. Though there are no alpine areas in the park, a few alpine plants isolated on the highest peaks, such as mountain avens and stiff gentian, have persisted in the specialized habitat of high-elevation cliff faces.

Because of the tremendous elevational range in the park—from 875 feet to 6,643 feet at the top of Clingmans Dome—there is a wide variety of soil and climatic microsites. Thus, trees that are common in northern New England can find a home here, along with southern species prevalent in Florida. The mountainous topography also plays a role in biodiversity, with north slopes cooler and shadier than south slopes, which are drier and warmer. Natural disturbances from wildfires, hurricanes, and ice storms also contribute to the mix.

Disease and competition with exotic species have taken a toll on the plant communities. Today, more than 21 percent of the vascular flora of the park is non-native. Other species, such as the chestnut, have suffered from disease. As a consequence of chestnut blight, there are no mature chestnut trees in the forest, though sprouts continue to grow from ancient root systems. One can appreciate the effect by comparing today's forest

Violets on the forest floor in Roaring Fork Valley.

composition with a survey done in 1905 that recorded chestnut trees as constituting 30 percent of the forests in the Cades Cove area. Similarly, the balsam woolly adelgid has largely killed off the Fraser fir, which once accounted for half the trees in the higher-elevation forests of the Smokies. And more than half the flowering dogwoods in the park have died from dogwood anthracnose, an introduced fungus that attacks the tree's leaves and branches, forming cankers that eventually kill the tree.

Human influences also play a role in the plant mosaic. Logging prior to the creation of the park removed many of the larger old-growth forest stands. Grazing on mountaintops helped create grassy balds. And protection in the park has left some virgin forest intact; this is where some of the greatest species diversity occurs. Indeed, GSMNP harbors the largest continuous stand of virgin timber in the eastern United States. The significance of this primary forest cannot be overstated. There are at least 175,000 acres of virgin forests in the Smokies. By comparison, in all of Maine, an area forty times as large, there are less than 36,000 acres of forest that have never been visited by an ax or a chain saw; most of this is subalpine spruce-fir forest in Baxter State Park. All these factors work together to create a continuously shifting vegetative mosaic in GSMNP.

Virgin or Old-Growth Forests

One of the most significant and valuable resources in GSMNP is its virgin forest. According to Park Service analysis, 35.9 percent of the park is uncut forestlands. Of this acreage, 38.7 percent is cove hardwood, 15.3 percent is northern hardwood, and 13.3 percent is mixed mesic hardwood; other types make up less than 10 percent of the mix.

There is tremendous scientific value to these reserves. Virgin forests often have different structures, plant associations, and characteristics from logged or otherwise disturbed forests. One comparison between logged and never-logged forests found that even eighty years after timber harvest, at least 50 percent of the ground flora species found in virgin forests were missing from the logged area. Another study found that the soil layer in logged forest had 50 percent less moisture than that in undisturbed forests. A third study estimated that salamander populations may require up to 120 years to recover from logging events. Other differences yet to be determined almost certainly exist.

Much of the virgin forestland in GSMNP would qualify as "old-growth" forest. Old-growth forests have certain characteristics not found

A hiker stands amidst virgin old growth. Cove hardwood forests have a surprisingly open understory that is easy to walk through.

in recently disturbed forests. First, as the name implies, there is an abundance of older trees. Indicators of age include general large size, a bole free of branches, furrowed bark, and even an abundance of snags or broken crowns. Indeed, dead snags are not a wasted resource; they may be even more important to the forest ecosystem than the living trees. Such snags and broken crowns are important for many wildlife species. Everything from woodpeckers to black bears depend on them for their homes and food resources.

In addition, old-growth forests have an abundance of fallen logs. These logs provide homes for amphibians such as salamanders, as well as small mammals such as voles and mice. When these logs fall into creeks, they

Dead trees are not a "wasted" resource but a critical part of the life cycle of a forest. Fallen logs provide a long-term supply of nutrients and a home for many forest creatures, including salamanders, small mammals such as voles, and countless species of insects and fungi.

provide homes for fish. Indeed, in smaller streams, more than 50 percent of the habitat structure is created by fallen boles. In GSMNP, streams in virgin forests have four times the volume of dead, downed wood found in previously logged sites. Even more striking is that streams in virgin forests have ten times more debris dams in streams (creating fish habitat) than logged sites do.

The fallen and dead trees create canopy gaps that are scattered throughout the forest. These small openings are important for the distribution of many forest floor species that cannot tolerate direct sunlight but still require more light than typically falls through an intact canopy. The holes in the canopy also provide a place for new plants to grow. Windthrow is typically responsible for many of these gaps in the canopy. Over time, the forest floor becomes potted and mounded by the upturned root wads and holes created when trees fall over. This creates a microtopography that results in diverse plant communities on the forest floor.

Old-growth forests also tend to have a multilayered forest canopy, with dominant primary trees in the highest canopy and many subdominant and shade-tolerant species layered beneath. A wide diversity of ages and species is also a hallmark of older tree stands.

Although these are the common characteristics of old-growth forests, they are not universal. For instance, some of the older pine stands in GSMNP, such as Table Mountain pine and pitch pine, tend to be dominated by single species.

At the time of settlement, some truly immense trees were found in the virgin Appalachian forests. The largest species were chestnut and yellow poplar (tulip tree). Historic records indicate that the largest poplars were 11 to 12 feet in diameter, up to 36 feet in circumference, and nearly 200 feet tall. Some hemlocks in West Virginia had 9-foot diameters. There are records of white pine in Pennsylvania reaching heights of 230 feet.

In the forests of GSMNP, there are huge trees that exceed sizes found elsewhere among their species. For instance, one red maple in the park is more than 23 feet in circumference and 135 feet tall. Yellow poplars in the park often grow 170 to 180 feet high and exceed 7 feet in diameter. There are red spruce with 14-foot girths. Although some of this size is a reflection of the exceptional growing conditions in the Great Smoky Mountains, some of these trees are also very old by eastern standards. At least one hemlock is known to be more than 500 years old.

A hiker stands by a giant yellow poplar. Such massive old-growth trees were once common in the southern Appalachians prior to the logging era.

One of the best places to see old-growth forest stands in GSMNP is the Ramsay Cascade Trail, which has some of the largest yellow poplars in the park. The Noland Divide Trail passes through virgin spruce forest. The Caldwell and Boogerman Trails in the Cataloochee drainage have significant old-growth forests, as do Laurel Falls Trail and Gregory Ridge Trail.

Forest Types

Pine-Oak Forest

Both pine and oak are better adapted to dry sites than are other forest tree species. There are two variations on these pine-oak forests: closed and open stands. The closed oak forests are found on dry, low- to mid-elevation slopes. They tend to be dominated by white, northern red, black, and chestnut oaks. Other associates include pignut hickory, red maple, yellow poplar, and black gum. Smaller trees include witch hazel and flowering dogwood and shrubs such as mountain laurel and flame azalea.

Open oak and pine stands are more common on ridges, particularly rocky outcrops. Common associated species include the previously mentioned oaks, as well as Table Mountain pine, pitch pine, Virginia pine, and scarlet oak. Pine-oak forest dominates rocky ridges and south-facing exposed sites, particularly on the west side of the park. Wildfire is especially common in these forest types and may be essential for the maintenance of some species. Over time, the sun-loving pines are usually overshadowed by the oaks. The stands then become essentially oak woodlands unless another disturbance opens up the canopy to favor the pines again. Only in extremely rocky or sandy areas are pines able to maintain their ecological foothold.

Hemlock Forest

Eastern hemlock loves moist, shady slopes and coves up to 4,000 feet, although it is occasionally found up to 5,000 feet. It is common along streams. Other trees often associated with hemlock are red maple, sugar maple, yellow birch, yellow poplar, Fraser magnolia, and striped maple. Understory shrubs such as rosebay rhododendron and witch hobble are common. The hike to Grotto Falls passes through some beautiful old-growth hemlock forest.

Cove Hardwood Forest

The ultimate expression of southern Appalachian forests is found in the cove hardwood sites. *Cove* refers to a sheltered basin or hillside where the soils are deep and moist. Most cove hardwood stands are found below 4,000 feet. Within GSMNP, many of the dominant species reach record size. For instance, there is a yellow birch with a 14-foot circumference,

Dogwood in old-growth cove hardwood forest. Cove hardwood forests support one of the richest diversity of trees and shrubs per acre found in the United States.

a yellow poplar more than 24 feet around, and a yellow buckeye that reaches 16 feet in circumference. Such giants are rare or nonexistent outside of GSMNP.

Dominant overstory trees include white basswood, Carolina silverbell, yellow poplar, yellow buckeye, sugar maple, red maple, yellow birch, white ash, eastern hemlock, and up to twenty other species. At one time, these forests were dominated by American chestnut, but chestnut blight has extirpated all mature trees from these forest stands. Chestnut sprouts still grow from stumps. Understory trees and shrubs include doghobble, hydrangea, redbud, sourwood, flowering dogwood, sassafras, and box elder. Hundreds of wildflowers are associated with the forest floor, including wood anemone, mayapple, wake-robin, white trillium, hepatica, wild geranium, foamflower, Dutchman's-pipe, false Solomon's seal, and ginseng. Good places to see representative cove hardwood forests include the Albright Grove Loop Trail, Ramsay Cascades Trail, and Cove Hardwood Nature Trail.

Northern Hardwood Forest

On the higher elevations of the Smokies, trees more typical of New England reach their southern range limits in the northern hardwood forest. Between 4,500 and 6,000 feet are such northern favorites as sugar maple, red maple, American beech, yellow birch, and yellow buckeye. Different species dominate these sites under different conditions. Yellow buckeye prevails in wet spots, and American beech is more common in drier sites. Shrubs include rosebay rhododendron, hobblebush, and smooth hydrangea. Flowers such as fawn lily, creeping bluet, wood sorrel, fringed phacelia, trillium, and beadlily are found.

Spruce-Fir Forest

The most restricted forest type found in GSMNP is the spruce-fir forest, occupying approximately 13,000 acres, or about 2 percent of the park area. It is restricted to elevations above 4,500 feet and is most common above 5,500 feet, where northern conditions similar to those in Canada occur. These forests dominate the Great Smoky Mountains high country in a nearly continuous belt 25 miles long from Clingmans Dome to Cosby Knob. The best examples of spruce-fir forest can be found on Clingmans Dome, Mount Guyot, Balsam Mountain, and Mount LeConte.

Spruce and fir shed snow well and can grow under extremely adverse conditions and in cold temperatures. The dominant species are evergreen

Fraser fir and red spruce. Spruce tends to grow at slightly lower elevations than does fir. The Fraser fir is a southern Appalachian endemic species that, unfortunately, is succumbing to balsam woolly adelgid, a non-native insect that is decimating fir stands throughout the region. Sometimes associated with these conifers are yellow birch, pin cherry, mountain maple, and mountain ash. Shrubs include Catawba and Carolina rhododendron, roundleaf gooseberry, Blueridge blueberry, hobblebush, and Allegheny menziesia. Flowers include painted trillium, pallid violet, wood sorrel, creeping bluet, and yellow beadlily.

Balds

Heath Balds

Heath balds occur throughout the higher elevations of GSMNP. Within the park, there are more than 475 balds of varying sizes. They are dominated by rhododendron species, including rosebay and Catawba. No one knows exactly how such balds came into existence or how they persist. Most ecologists believe that they were established by random fires and invaded by heath species that created such dense cover that other trees were unable to invade the site.

Grassy Balds

Grassy balds are generally found above 5,400 feet elevation. They are dominated by mountain oat grass, with thickets of flame azalea and serviceberry. These mountain meadows were used by settlers for grazing for many years. Now, in the absence of livestock, many are being invaded by trees. Two of the best grassy balds to visit are Gregory Bald and Andrew Bald.

Wildflowers

As impressive as GSMNP trees may be, they are rivaled by the park's spectacular wildflower blooms. The earliest-blooming flowers are spring ephemerals. Ephemerals appear in March and April, before the leaves on canopy trees block out the sun. They sprout, flower, and set seed all within a few months. Early in the season, soil moisture is high, along with nutrients and light, and spring ephemerals are designed to take advantage of this gold mine of critical growing conditions. Many of these spring blooms are found in the cove hardwood forests.

Rhododendron on Andrews Bald. Balds are found throughout the park. Their origins remain unclear. While some were created by fires and livestock grazing by settlers, others appear to be self sustaining.

Several other special habitats are well known for their wildflower displays. The spruce-fir zone contains northern species such as wood sorrel and bluebead lily, which reach their southern limits in GSMNP.

Geology also plays a role in plant distribution. The park's limestone-dominated basins of Cades Cove and Rich Mountain Gap include species such as blazing star, yellow mandarin, and bittersweet, which are attracted to such rock types.

Threats to the Flora

Most people presume that national parks protect the plants and animals within their borders. But despite the loving care provided by the National Park Service and the millions of visitors who enjoy the park while respecting the landscape, the plant communities in GSMNP are under assault. The most difficult problem is presented by non-native invaders—plants, animals, and diseases. Alien plants such as dandelion and Saint-John's-wort can outcompete native species for water, nutrients, and light. Alien animals are another problem. Feral hogs, also known as wild boars, escaped from a North Carolina game farm and now roam the southern Appalachians, including the park. Their rooting behavior has destroyed acres of wildflowers and other plants in the park. Alien diseases and insects are even more difficult to control, as evidenced by chestnut blight, the near extirpation of Fraser fir by the balsam woolly adelgid, and the growing threat from dogwood anthracnose.

The last major threat is the least appreciated and perhaps the most intolerable, because it could be readily corrected. Air pollution is now recognized as a major factor in the tragic death of forest stands across the eastern United States. Pollutants, from coal-fired power plants, combined with ozone pollution from auto exhaust, are killing off our forests. The irony is that technological solutions exist but are not being implemented because of an intractable but powerful coalition of coal-mining companies, coal-producing states, and power companies. These pollutants produce acid rainfall that bathes trees in a highly acidic fog and moisture for weeks or months at a time. These acid baths weaken trees, making them more susceptible to stress from insects, disease, or weather. Furthermore, the acid precipitation leaches aluminum and other heavy metals from soils, and they are taken up by plants, with lethal consequences.

Species Accounts

Coniferous Trees

Typically known as evergreens, conifers are cone-bearing species such as pine and spruce. They are usually well adapted to adverse growing conditions and tend to dominate cold, snowy regions or harsh, dry, droughty areas such as rocky ledges or sandy soils. The one exception to this generalization is the eastern hemlock, a species common in deep, rich soils. Nevertheless, the hemlock is still adapted to adversity and tolerates shade better than most trees do.

EASTERN WHITE PINE
(Pinus strobus)

Description. Height to 100 feet or more. Branches nearly horizontal. Needles 4 inches long in bundles of five. Cones 4 to 8 inches and slender. Bark dark gray and furrowed.

Distribution. Found from lowest elevations to about 5,000 feet. Large white pines are commonly encountered in Cades Cove.

Remarks. This is the largest pine in the Smokies. It is more common in northern states from Minnesota to Maine and reaches its southern limits along the Appalachian spine.

Old-growth white pine. Pines tend to grow on drier sites, and many are dependent on natural clearing events such as fire.

PITCH PINE
(Pinus rigida)

Description. Height to 50 feet. Crown broad and irregular. Yellowish green needles 4 inches long in bundles of three. Bark brown-gray and broken in plates. Cones egg shaped, 2 to 3 inches with stiff scales (giving rise to its Latin name *rigida*).

Distribution. Rocky soils below 4,000 feet.

Remarks. This pine prefers open, sunny sites and tends to grow on rocky ledges or invade after fires.

SHORTLEAF PINE
(Pinus echinata)

Description. Height to 90 feet. Rounded crown. Needles 2.5 inches, typically with two to three per bundle. Cones 1.5 inches, squat, egg shaped, with prickles on the ends of the open scales. Reddish bark deeply furrowed with pitch pockets.

Distribution. Ridge tops and dry slopes below 4,000 feet.

Remarks. The straight trunk of this species made it a favorite for ship masts.

VIRGINIA PINE
(*Pinus virginiana*)

Description. Height to 40 feet. Branches tend to droop. Needles stiff, 1.5 to 3 inches, with two to a bundle. Cones egg shaped, 1.5 to 2.5 inches long, typically growing in groups of two. Bark red-brown, in platelike strips typically three to four times as long as they are broad. Often assumes a shrubby growth form.
Distribution. Found in old fields and on poor soils below 3,000 feet.
Remarks. Turkeys, songbirds, and squirrels consume the seeds of this species.

TABLE MOUNTAIN PINE
(*Pinus pungens*)

Description. Height to 40 feet. Needles stiff and sharp pointed, generally 1.5 to 3 inches, with two per bundle. Closed cones 2 to 3 inches long and armed with stout spines, typically growing in clusters of two or more. Cones may remain on trees for up to twenty years. Bark is red-brown and separated in irregular plates.
Distribution. Rocky ridges and dry slopes. Most common between 3,000 and 4,500 feet. Often forms pure stands.
Remarks. This southern Appalachian endemic benefits from fire, which causes its cones to open and shed seeds and eliminates competition from other trees.

EASTERN HEMLOCK
(*Tsuga canadensis*)

Description. Height to 100 feet. Pyramid shaped with drooping branches. Needles flat, soft, and flexible, usually 0.5 inch in length. Two parallel white lines on underside of needles. Cones 0.75 inch and brown. Bark brown and furrowed.
Distribution. Likes moist, shady locations along streams, in ravines, and on north slopes between 3,500 and 5,000 feet.
Remarks. The largest hemlock in the United States is found in the park. It is 165 feet tall and more than 16 feet in circumference.

EASTERN RED CEDAR
(*Juniperus virginiana*)

Description. Height to 40 feet. Lacy, scalelike leaves somewhat linear or needlelike. Prickly to the touch. Fruit 0.5 inch, round, and berrylike, but hard greenish blue. Bark grayish brown in fibrous strips.
Distribution. Prefers limestone soils below 2,000 feet. Most common in Cades Cove and Whiteoak Sink.
Remarks. Many wildlife species feed on "juniper" berries, including cedar waxwings, wild turkey, raccoons, and rabbits.

FRASER FIR
(Abies fraseri)

Description. Height to 60 feet. Pyramid shaped with branches in whorls. Needles dark green above and silvery white below, flat, 0.5 to 1 inch, with notched tips attached directly to branches. Cones 2 to 3 inches with yellow-green bracts held upright on branches. Bark gray and smooth, marked by blister resins.
Distribution. Found at the highest elevations between 4,500 and 6,642 feet, often associated with red spruce.
Remarks. A southern Appalachian endemic, with the majority of all known stands found within GSMNP. The balsam woolly adelgid, an exotic insect introduced from Europe, has killed 95 percent of all mature Fraser firs in the park.

RED SPRUCE
(Picea rubens)

Description. Height to 80 feet. Narrow conical crown. Needles 0.5 inch and pointed. Prickly to the touch. Cones 1 to 2 inches with smooth-margined scales. Bark dark brown to gray and broken into irregularly shaped flakes.
Distribution. Most common above 4,000 feet and up to 6,642 feet.
Remarks. Spruce are being destroyed by acid precipitation caused by pollution from power plants.

Witch hobble and red spruce in mist. Red spruce, a common species in New England, reaches its southern limits in the Great Smoky Mountains.

Deciduous Trees

Deciduous or hardwood trees shed their leaves each fall and regrow new ones each spring. Deciduous trees grow best in areas with an abundance of moisture.

RED MAPLE
(Acer rubrum)

Description. Height to 90 feet. Crown rounded. Leaves opposite, typically palm shaped, with V-shaped notch between lobes, about 5 inches across and toothed. Bark dark gray and furrowed.
Distribution. Throughout the park, from lowest elevations to 6,000 feet.
Remarks. One of the most abundant trees in GSMNP.

Red maple leaves on fern near Cataloochee Divide. Northern species such as sugar maple are common in the middle and higher elevations of the park.

SUGAR MAPLE
(Acer saccharum)

Description. Height to 80 feet. Broad rounded crown. Leaves opposite, 5 inches, with few-toothed lobes. Bark gray and deeply furrowed. Leaves have U-shaped space between lobes.
Distribution. Generally found below 5,000 feet. Dominant tree in cove hardwood, northern hardwood, and hemlock forests.
Remarks. The Sugarlands in GSMNP gets its name from the formerly abundant sugar maples found there, which were tapped to make maple sugar.

STRIPED MAPLE
(Acer pensylvanicum)

Description. Height to 50 feet, but generally smaller. Leaves 4 to 5 inches wide with three lobes, finely toothed. Bark green with chalky white lines.
Distribution. Fairly common, particularly below 4,000 feet. Typically an understory tree found in cove hardwood, northern hardwood, and even spruce-fir forests.
Remarks. Nicknamed "goose foot maple" for the shape of its leaf. A record striped maple found along Trillium Gap Trail measured 77 feet.

YELLOW BUCKEYE
(Aesculus octandra)

Description. Height to 80 feet. Crown rounded. Leaves palmlike, compound, with five to seven leaflets. Bark dark gray-brown, generally smooth or with flattened plates. Bears cluster of 1-inch yellow flowers. Fruit 3-inch leathery spheres.
Distribution. Deep soils at 1,000 to 6,000 feet. Dominant tree in cove hardwood and northern hardwood forests, but occasionally found in spruce-fir forests.
Remarks. Can grow from root sprouts. One of the first trees to leaf out in spring.

YELLOW BIRCH
(Betula alleghaniensis)

Description. Height to 100 feet. Crown rounded to cylindrical. Leaves 3 to 5 inches, sharply toothed and pointed. Bark yellowish bronze, peeling in strips. Fruit pineconelike, 1 to 1.5 inches.
Distribution. One of the most common trees between 3,500 and 5,000 feet, particularly in northern hardwood forests, but found from 1,200 feet up to 6,400 feet.
Remarks. The bark is loaded with resins that make it a good fire starter.

BITTERNUT HICKORY
(Carya cordiformis)

Description. Height to 60 feet. Crown broad and spreading. Compound leaves 6 to 8 inches, with seven to nine leaflets on each leaf. Bark smooth.
Distribution. Common along streams below 3,000 feet.
Remarks. One of the fastest-growing hickory species.

AMERICAN CHESTNUT
(Castanea dentata)

Description. Height to 20 feet before dying. Leaves 5 to 10 inches with sharp teeth. Nuts have spiny skin.
Distribution. Once a dominant tree below 5,000 feet. Still occurs as root sprouts.
Remarks. The American chestnut was once one of the most common and magnificent trees in the cove hardwood forests, but chestnut blight has killed all mature trees. One tree in GSMNP measured more than 33 feet in circumference.

AMERICAN BEECH
(*Fagus grandifolia*)

Description. Height to 120 feet. Crown narrow, but rounded. Leaves 5 to 6 inches, ovate, with prominent toothed margins. Bark light gray and smooth. Fruit spiny burs. Trees tend to retain brown leaves all winter long.
Distribution. Common to nearly 6,000 feet. Dominant in cove hardwood and northern hardwood forests.
Remarks. At higher elevations, sometimes forms nearly pure stands called "beech gaps."

WHITE ASH
(*Fraxinus americana*)

Description. Height to 90 feet. Crown pyramidal. Leaves up to 6 inches and pinnately compound, with seven leaflets. Bark dark brown and fissured.
Distribution. Up to 5,000 feet. Common in moist woodlands.
Remarks. Ash is the wood of choice for baseball bats, ax handles, and oars.

Silverbell in bloom.

CAROLINA SILVERBELL
(*Halesia carolina*)

Description. Height to 30 feet. Leaves 3 to 5 inches, oval to elliptical, with fine-toothed margins and sharp points. Bark light gray in young trees to reddish brown in older ones. Flowers bell-like, white, sometimes pinkish; appear in spring before the leaves unfold.
Distribution. Common to 5,000 feet.
Remarks. Typically a smallish tree, but the national champion silverbell is found in the park and exceeds 100 feet.

BLACK WALNUT
(Juglans nigra)

Description. Height to 90 feet. Leaves 12 to 24 inches long and pinnately compound. Leaflets 2 to 4 inches, finely toothed, and pointed. Bark dark brown and deeply fissured. Fruit 1.5 to 2 inches and globular, with a fine point at the apex.
Distribution. Found below 3,500 feet, usually associated with old homesteads.
Remarks. Mountain people used black walnut for gun stocks, furniture, and rafters.

SWEETGUM
(Liquidambar styraciflua)

Description. Height to 80 feet. Leaves 5 to 7 inches wide and star shaped, with five pointed lobes. Bark light gray, often deeply furrowed. Fruit round, 1 to 1.5 inches, with burs.
Distribution. Common along streams below 2,000 feet.
Remarks. Crushed leaves have a sweet smell—hence the name sweetgum.

YELLOW POPLAR
(*Liriodendron tulipifera*)

Description. Height to 200 feet, 8 to 10 feet in diameter. Leaves 5 inches across with four large lobes. Bark light gray and furrowed on older trees. Flowers 1.5 to 3 inches and yellow-green.
Distribution. Streamsides and rich soils below 4,000 feet. One of the most common trees in GSMNP.
Remarks. Also called tulip tree. One of the largest hardwoods in the southern Appalachians.

FRASER MAGNOLIA
(*Magnolia fraseri*)

Description. Height to 50 feet. Crown spreading. Leaves 16 inches, widening toward a tip with a notch at the base. Bark grayish brown and relatively smooth. Flowers up to 9 inches across, cream colored, fragrant.
Distribution. Moist areas up to 5,000 feet.
Remarks. Originally discovered by botanist William Bartram, who surveyed the South for plants as early as the 1770s.

UMBRELLA MAGNOLIA
(*Magnolia tripetala*)

Description. Height to 35 feet. Crown spreading. Leaves 18 to 20 inches, obovate. Bark light gray, relatively smooth. Flowers 9 inches, cup shaped, white. Unpleasant odor.
Distribution. Common in rich soils along streams below 2,500 feet. Particularly abundant in Cades Cove and along Abrams Creek and Little River.
Remarks. Peak bloom of this beautiful blossom is in early May.

BLACKGUM
(*Nyssa sylvatica*)

Description. Height to 130 feet. Crown rounded, branches horizontal relative to trunk. Leaves 5 inches and oblong, with wavy edges and pointed tip. Bark light brown and furrowed into squares. Fruit berrylike, 0.5 inch, blue-black.
Distribution. Common on dry sites at low to middle elevations, particularly among oaks and pines.
Remarks. Also known as black tupelo. Berries are avidly sought by wildlife. In autumn, the blood red leaves are particularly attractive.

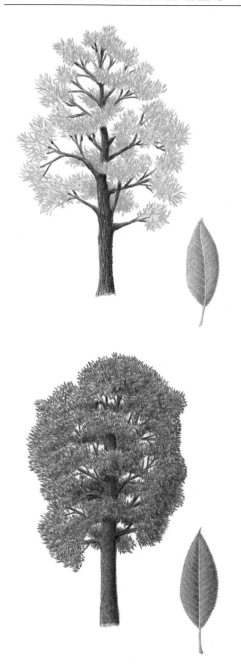

SOURWOOD
(Oxydendrum arboreum)

Description. Height to 50 feet. Crown narrow and somewhat conical. Leaves lancelike, 6 inches, fine toothed along margins. Bark shiny gray to brown. Flowers urn shaped and white, growing along a long, curved axis.
Distribution. Common in drier sites among oaks and pines below 4,500 feet.
Remarks. Leaves have a sour taste, as the name implies. Flowers attract numerous bees and are a source for superb honey.

BLACK CHERRY
(Prunus serotina)

Description. Height to 100 feet. Crown rounded. Leaves 2 to 6 inches, oblong, pointed. Leaf margins finely toothed. Flowers white in clusters. Fruit dark red. Bark reddish, smooth when young and scaly when older.
Distribution. Common below 5,000 feet, particularly in cove hardwood forests.
Remarks. Largest of the wild cherries in the United States.

WHITE OAK
(Quercus alba)

Description. Height to 90 feet. Crown rounded with wide-spreading branches. Leaves 7 inches, with five to nine rounded lobes. Bark light gray and scaly. Acorns 1 inch.
Distribution. Most common oak in GSMNP. More abundant at lower elevations and on moister sites than other oaks.
Remarks. White oak acorns are important wildlife food.

SCARLET OAK
(Quercus coccinea)

Description. Height to 80 feet. Crown open. Leaves 7 inches, shiny, with seven to nine deep lobes and toothed tips. Bark dark gray and furrowed in plates. Acorns 1 inch.
Distribution. Common on drier sites, often with pines, below 3,500 feet.
Remarks. Leaves turn scarlet in autumn—hence its name.

SOUTHERN RED OAK
(Quercus falcata)

Description. Height to 100 feet. Crown rounded with wide-spreading branches. Leaves 8 inches, broadly oval, with three to seven deep lobes with bristles on the tips. Leaf underside has feltlike hairs. Bark dark brown and fissured. Acorns 0.5 inch.
Distribution. Mostly found below 2,500 feet with pines and other oaks.
Remarks. Leaf has a long middle "finger" that helps distinguish it from other oaks.

CHESTNUT OAK
(Quercus prinus)

Description. Height to 70 feet. Leaves 4 to 8 inches, oval, roughly toothed. Undersides of leaves are hairy. Bark reddish brown. Acorns 1.5 inches.
Distribution. Dry rocky ridges below 4,000 feet, as well as among other hardwoods.
Remarks. The large acorns are a major food source for wildlife, including bears, deer, and squirrels.

NORTHERN RED OAK
(Quercus rubra)

Description. Height to 80 feet. Crown rounded with stout, spreading branches. Leaves 8 inches, with seven to eleven shallow lobes tipped with bristles. Bark dark gray and furrowed. Acorns 1 inch.
Distribution. Up to 6,000 feet. Grows on moister sites than most other oaks do. Reaches greatest abundance at mid elevations.
Remarks. One of the largest oaks in GSMNP. A northern species that reaches its southern limit in the park.

BLACK LOCUST
(Robinia pseudoacacia)

Description. Height to 60 feet. Crown irregular. Trunk often crooked. Leaves 10 inches, pinnately compound with seven to nineteen oval 1-inch leaflets. Thorns 0.5 inch in pairs on twigs. Bark light gray and furrowed. Flowers pealike, white, in drooping clusters.
Distribution. Grows in disturbed sites from low to mid elevations.
Remarks. Wood resists rot and was used by settlers for fences and foundations.

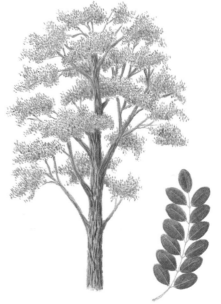

SASSAFRAS
(Sassafras albidum)

Description. Height to 90 feet. Crown open and flat with spreading branches. Leaves 6 inches, shape varies, but often lobed, somewhat mitten-shaped. Bark reddish brown. Fruit berry-like, blue-black.

Distribution. Disturbed sites such as abandoned fields, typically below 4,500 feet.

Remarks. The berries are a favorite food of birds and other wildlife.

WHITE BASSWOOD
(Tilia americana var. *heterophylla)*

Description. Height to 80 feet. Crown rounded, dense. Leaves 5 inches, heart shaped, coarsely toothed. Bark gray, furrowed. Flowers cream colored in clusters.

Distribution. Cove hardwood forests from 3,000 to 5,000 feet.

Remarks. Bees swarm to basswood flowers, a source of exceptional honey.

AMERICAN ELM
(*Ulmus americana*)

Description. Height to 90 feet. Crown vase shaped. Leaves 5 inches, toothed. Leaf base asymmetrical. Bark gray, furrowed.
Distribution. Common along streams and on other moist soils below 2,000 feet.
Remarks. One of the most beautiful shade trees in North America. Many have succumbed to the fungus that causes Dutch elm disease.

SERVICEBERRY
(*Amelanchier arborea*)

Description. Height to 25 feet. Leaves 3 to 5 inches, finely toothed. Flowers white, star shaped. Fruit is a purple berry.
Distribution. Common to 6,000 feet. Found as understory of cove hardwoods and along the edges of balds.
Remarks. Also known as shadbush.

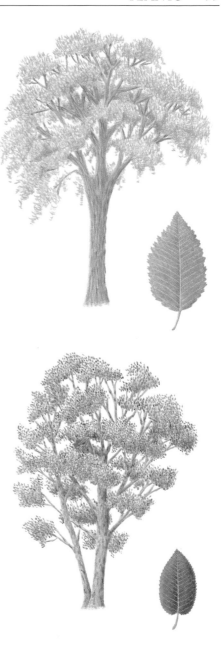

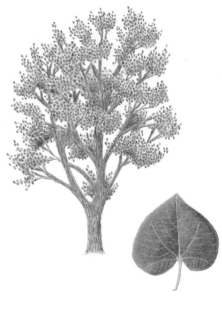

EASTERN REDBUD
(Cercis canadensis)

Description. Height to 30 feet. Shrubby tree with spreading crown. Leaves 5 inches, heart shaped. Flowers 0.5 inch, in pink clusters that appear before leaves.
Distribution. Most common in the western part of the park on limestone-dominated soils, including Cades Cove, Cosby, and Foothills Parkway.
Remarks. Often used as an ornamental tree in yards.

FLOWERING DOGWOOD
(Cornus florida)

Description. Height to 40 feet. Crown rounded. Leaves 4 inches, opposite. Bark gray, fissured in 1-inch squares. Flowers 4 inches, with four white, petal-like bracts. Fruit is a bright red berry.
Distribution. Once common below 3,000 feet.
Remarks. Dogwood was once one of the most abundant low-elevation trees. Unfortunately, a fungus is killing it off throughout its range.

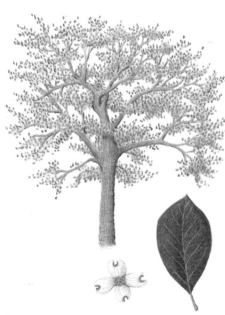

FLAME AZALEA
(*Rhododendron calendulaceum*)

Description. Height to 10 feet. Erect shrub. Leaves 2.5 inches, elliptical, finely toothed. Flowers 1 inch; trumpet shaped; bright orange, salmon, white, pink, and yellow.

Distribution. Up to 6,000 feet, in open pine and oak forests.

Remarks. Reaches peak bloom on Andrews Bald in mid-June.

Flame azalea.

MOUNTAIN LAUREL
(*Kalmia latifolia*)

Description. Height to 10 feet. Many-stemmed shrub. Leaves 3 inches, evergreen. Bark rusty. Flowers 0.75 inch, saucer shaped, white to pink.
Distribution. Cove hardwood forests, oak woodlands, and balds.
Remarks. One of the most abundant shrubs on heath balds.

Mountain laurel.

ROSEBAY RHODODENDRON
(Rhododendron maximum)

Description. Height to 15 feet. Large, thicket-forming shrub. Leaves 6 inches, oblong, evergreen. Flowers showy, 1.5 inches, white or pink.
Distribution. Common throughout the park up to 5,000 feet and occasionally higher. Prefers moist sites.
Remarks. Peak bloom is mid-June.

CATAWBA RHODODENDRON
(Rhododendron catawbiense)

Description. Height to 15 feet. Dense shrub with rounded crown. Leaves 5 inches, evergreen, leathery, with a round base and blunt tip. Flowers 2.5 inches, bell shaped, pink to purple.
Distribution. Heath balds generally above 4,000 feet.
Remarks. A southern Appalachian endemic that blooms in early to mid-June.

Flowers

TRAILING ARBUTUS
(Epigaea repens)

Description. Low, woody shrub. White blooms, 0.5 inch.
Distribution. Dry oak-pine forests and heath balds.
Remarks. One of the earliest blooming flowers, March to April.

BLOODROOT
(Sanguinaria canadensis)

Description. Height to 10 inches. Narrow white petals surrounding yellow stamens. Leaves deeply lobed, 4 to 7 inches.
Distribution. Moist woods.
Remarks. Blooms March to April.

TOOTHWORT
(Cardamine diphylla)

Description. Height 8 to 12 inches. Leaves three-parted and opposite. Flowers in small terminal cluster, white, 0.5 to 1 inch, with four petals and four sepals.
Distribution. Moist woods with deep soils.
Remarks. Blooms April to May. This plant was thought to cure toothaches—hence its common name.

SHARP-LOBED HEPATICA
(Hepatica acutiloba)

Description. Height 3 to 6 inches. Flowers pinkish white, 0.5 to 1 inch. Leaves have three lobes with distinctly pointed tips.
Distribution. Low- to mid-elevation moist woods.
Remarks. Early blooming, March to April.

MAYAPPLE
(Podophyllum peltatum)

Description. Height 12 to 18 inches. Flowers white, nodding, 1 to 2 inches, solitary with waxy petals. Umbrellalike leaves.
Distribution. Moist hardwood forests.
Remarks. Blooms April to June.

FRINGED PHACELIA
(Phacelia fimbriata)

Description. Height to 6 inches. Flowers 0.5 inch, white, cuplike, with fringed petals. Produces dense clusters of blossoms. Leaves alternate, 2 inches, with triangular lobes.
Distribution. Mid- to high-elevation moist woods.
Remarks. Blooms March to May. This is a winter annual that disappears soon after blooming in early spring.

Fringed phacelia is a common spring flower.

Trillium in bloom.

WHITE TRILLIUM
(*Trillium grandiflorum*)

Description. Height 10 to 18 inches. Flowers have three large, white petals 2 to 4 inches long. Leaves in whorls of three.
Distribution. Low- to mid-elevation moist woods and coves.
Remarks. Blooms April to May.

WOOLLY BLUE VIOLET
(*Viola sororia*)

Description. Height to 10 inches. Blue flowers up to 1 inch across, borne on leafless flower stalks. Flowers often woolly—hence the name. Leaves heart shaped, arising from a basal cluster.
Distribution. Moist and dry woods at low to mid elevations.
Remarks. Blooms March to April.

TURK'S CAP LILY
(Lilium superbum)

Description. Height to 7 feet. Showy orange, nodding flowers 5 inches across. Petals and sepals turn back on themselves. Lance-shaped leaves with prominent veins.
Distribution. Moist woodlands, balds, and shrubby areas at all elevations.
Remarks. Blooms July to September.

BLUETS
(Houstonia serpyllifolia)

Description. Height 3 to 5 inches. Four blue petals make up flower that is about 0.3 inch across. Oblong basal leaves.
Distribution. Moist woodlands and along streams at all elevations.
Remarks. Blooms May to August.

RED COLUMBINE
(Aquilegia canadensis)

Description. Height to 2 feet. Long red spurs hang down from stems; red sepals cover yellow petals. Leaves divided into lobed leaflets.
Distribution. Found at all elevations, mostly on rocky cliffs and rocky slopes.
Remarks. Blooms April to June. *Aquilegia* is Latin for "eagle."

FIRE PINK
(Silene virginica)

Description. Height to 2 feet. Bright red flowers 1.5 inches across, with a notch at the end. Loosely formed clusters atop slender stems. Leaves slender and opposite.
Distribution. Dry rocky slopes.
Remarks. Blooms April to June. Hummingbirds are one of the major pollinators.

TROUT LILY
(Erythronium americanum)

Description. Height to 12 inches. Six yellow petals and sepals bent backward. Linear leaves narrow at the base, up to 8 inches and spotted.
Distribution. Found in moist woods at all elevations, but most common in spruce-fir forests.
Remarks. Blooms April to June.

CARDINAL FLOWER
(Lobelia cardinalis)

Description. Height to 5 feet. Flowers cardinal red, 1.5 inches across. Upper lip has two lobes; lower lip has three. Leaves lanceolate and toothed.
Distribution. Springs, seeps, and other moist areas.
Remarks. Blooms July to October.

YELLOW LADY'S SLIPPER
(Cypripedium pubescens)

Description. Height to 2 feet. Pouchlike yellow flower. Leaves lanceolate, up to 6 inches.
Distribution. Moist woodlands at low to mid elevations.
Remarks. Blooms April to June.

FALSE HELLEBORE
(Veratrum viride)

Description. Height to 8 feet. Large, dense cluster of yellow-green flowers. Leaves very large, with prominent parallel veins.
Distribution. Seeps, wet meadows, and moist thickets at high elevations.
Remarks. Blooms May to June. Poisonous to eat.

PINK LADY'S SLIPPER
(Cypripedium acaule)

Description. Height to 20 inches. Flowers possess a pink pouch that some say resembles a moccasin. Stems leafless. Leaves basal.
Distribution. Bogs and dry woods.
Remarks. Blooms April to July.

WOOD SORREL
(Oxalis montana)

Description. Height to 6 inches. Flowers white with pink lines. Leaves shamrock shaped.
Distribution. Moist woods in the spruce-fir zone.
Remarks. Blooms June to July.

Ferns

BRACKEN FERN
(Pteridium aquilinum)

Description. Height to 24 inches. Stalks erect and stiff. Fronds divided into three broadly triangular leaflets that are sub-divided two to three times into leaflets.
Distribution. Dry habitats, roadsides, open meadows.
Remarks. Frequently invades burned areas.

CINNAMON FERN
(Osmunda cinnamomea)

Description. Height to 4 feet. Woolly cinnamon brown stalks. Large, gracefully arching fronds, bipinnate, with oblong, lobed leaflets. Grows in circular clumps.
Distribution. Streamsides and bogs.
Remarks. Spring fiddleheads are covered with silvery hairs.

SENSITIVE FERN
(Onoclea sensibilis)

Description. Height to 24 inches. Stalks very brittle. Fronds leathery, pinnate, with wavy, opposite lobes.
Distribution. Moist woods and seep areas.
Remarks. One of the earliest ferns to be killed by frost.

CHRISTMAS FERN
(Polystichum acrostichoides)

Description. Height to 20 inches. Stalks stout and scaly. Evergreen fronds pinnate with lanceolate, toothed leaflets. Each leaflet has an earlike projection at the base.
Distribution. Moist woods, ravines, and streamsides.
Remarks. Fertile fronds grow taller and straighter than sterile ones.

FISH

The southern Appalachian Mountains—in particular, the Tennessee River system, which drains GSMNP—have one of the most diverse native fish populations in the entire United States. More than seventy species of fish have been recorded in the park—one of the highest numbers among similarly sized U.S. parks. Most of the fish in the park are small "minnows" or species that are little known. In many cases, only a tiny amount about their natural history is known. At least twenty fish species found in GSMNP are relegated to the lower portion of Abrams Creek and nowhere else in the park, although they may be found elsewhere in the region. A few species of "game" fish, such as brook trout, are better known.

In many cases, past human land uses and management practices have created problems for the park's native fisheries. The brook trout, for instance, has suffered significant declines due to competition with non-native fish such as the rainbow trout, which were stocked in streams to improve fishing opportunities. Brook trout also suffered from past logging and agricultural practices that diminished water quality. Today, the species is facing a new threat—air pollution that is acidifying the small headwater streams where this native jewel is found. The brook trout in GSMNP are genetically unique, distinct from brook trout in New England or those found in hatchery populations. As one of the major refugia for brook trout as well as other native fish in the East, GSMNP's role in preserving biodiversity grows more important each year as fish species face greater threats to their existence.

Species Accounts

Lampreys

Lampreys are descendants of the oldest known fish. They lack the scales, bones, jaws, and paired fins of regular fish. Lampreys have circular suction-disk mouths with rasping teeth. Some are parasitic, latching on to other fish and sucking out body fluids. Three species have been recorded in GSMNP, but only one is described here.

MOUNTAIN BROOK LAMPREY
(Ichtyomyzon greeleyi)

Description. Length to 7.75 inches. Gray-brown to olive on back; white or cream below. Slightly notched dorsal fin.
Distribution. Gravel riffles and clean, high-gradient waterways.
Remarks. Mountain brook lampreys are nonparasitic and do not feed after transformation into adults.

Minnows

Included are members of the family Cyprinidae, the largest group of fish in North America. This group includes shiners, chubs, and daces. These small fish are among the most abundant fish species in eastern North American streams. One trait that may contribute to their success is the habit of laying eggs in crevices, making it difficult for other fish to eat them. Males of some species tend to be brightly colored. Twenty-seven species have been recorded in GSMNP.

WHITETAIL SHINER
(Cyprinella galactura)

Description. Length to 6 inches. Small eyes. Two large white areas on caudal fin base; black blotch on back of dorsal fin. Slender body. Dark olive back, silver sides. Breeding male has blue back and sides with red tint near anal fin.
Distribution. Clear, boulder-strewn, headwater streams of the Tennessee River drainage.
Remarks. Crevice spawner—females deposit eggs in cracks in rocks or submerged logs.

FLAME CHUB
(Hemitremia flammea)

Description. Length to 2.75 inches. Chubby with a short head, short snout, and round eye. Olive above; dark stripe along back; dark streaks along upper side, then light stripe, then black stripe, ending in black caudal spot. Large individuals, particularly males, may have red along the bottom third of the body.
Distribution. Restricted in GSMNP to a few springs and spring-fed streams on the western side of the park.
Remarks. Rare over much of its range due to habitat destruction.

WARPAINT SHINER
(*Luxilus coccogenis*)

Description. Length to 5.5 inches. Black band on yellow dorsal fin; black edge on caudal fin. Olive above; dark stripe along middle of back; large black bar behind gill cover on silver side. Breeding male has red side, red snout, and red on dorsal fin.

Distribution. In Tennessee River drainage headwaters where there is fast water with gravel and riffles.

Remarks. Named for the breeding males, whose bright colors are said to resemble war paint.

BIGEYE CHUB
(*Hybopsis amblops*)

Description. Length to 3.5 inches. Large eye. Small mouth. Olive on back; silver sides with a black stripe. Slender, compressed body.

Distribution. Clear, clean, silt-free waters with rocky pools and current in the Tennessee River drainage.

Remarks. Sight feeder that collects invertebrates from clean, sandy bottoms.

Suckers

Suckers are differentiated from other fish by their large, thick lips and lack of teeth in the jaws. They tend to vacuum invertebrates from stream bottoms—hence their name. Six species have been recorded in GSMNP, but only one is discussed here.

SHORTHEAD REDHORSE
(*Moxostoma macrolepidotum*)

Description. Length to 29 inches. Stout body. Short head. Small mouth. Golden yellow on sides, with a white belly. Moderately forked caudal fin is often red.
Distribution. Prefers larger rivers with moderate flow over gravel or rock bottoms.
Remarks. Females tend to be larger than males.

Catfish

Catfish, including bullheads and madtoms, makes up the largest family of fish in North America north of Mexico. Members of this family have four pairs of barbels or whiskers, no scales, and stout spines where the dorsal and pectoral fins would be. Most are active at night. Most of the madtoms are rare and endangered; several, including the yellowfin madtom and Smoky madtom, are part of a park reintroduction program.

YELLOW BULLHEAD
(*Ameiurus natalis*)

Description. Length to 12 inches. White or yellow chin whiskers (barbels). Long anal fin. Sawlike teeth on pectoral spine. Yellow-olive to nearly black above, fading to yellow-olive on sides; bright yellow or white below.
Distribution. Sluggish clear waters with rocky or gravel bottoms.
Remarks. Parents guard eggs and juveniles until they are about 2 inches long.

Trout

Trout are popular cold-water game fish. They tend to have small scales and streamlined bodies. Several varieties of fish are grouped under the collective name "trout," including the rainbow trout, which is really a salmon; the brown trout, which is a true trout; and the brook trout, which is a char. These names merely point out the different evolutionary heritage of these fish. Only the brook trout is native to the southern Appalachians. The others were stocked in the early days of the park to provide additional fishing opportunities. An effort to restore native brook trout habitat and populations is ongoing.

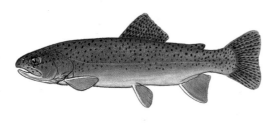

RAINBOW TROUT
(*Oncorhynchus mykiss*)

Description. Length to 45 inches (though never that large in GSMNP). Small, irregular black spots on back and most fins. Back steel blue; greenish to silver on sides, with pink to red stripe; white belly.
Distribution. Colder streams and rivers.
Remarks. Rainbow trout are native to the western United States and were introduced into GSMNP.

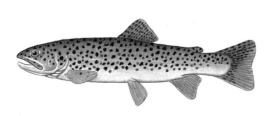

BROWN TROUT
(*Salmo trutta*)

Description. Length to 40 inches (though never that large in GSMNP). Red and black spots on head and body, with yellowish brown background. White to yellowish below.
Distribution. Clean, cool waters. Can tolerate slightly warmer temperatures than other trout, so tends to be found in lower reaches of trout streams.
Remarks. Native to Europe and introduced into the United States.

Brook trout are the only native trout to GSMNP. They are genetically distinct from other brook trout populations in the East. These natives are threatened by past stocking programs that have introduced exotic fish into the park, as well as by growing acidity of headwater streams due to air pollution from power plants and other sources.

BROOK TROUT
(Salvelinus fontinalis)

Description. Length to 27 inches (though considerably smaller in GSMNP). Slightly forked to nearly straight tail. Light green wavy lines or blotches on back. Blue halos around red spots on sides. Black line behind white edge on red lower fins.

Distribution. Native to all streams in GSMNP. Typically restricted to head-water areas.

Remarks. The brook trout of the southern Appalachians are genetically distinct from brook trout farther north in New York, New England, and Canada. Efforts are being made to restore brook trout to park waters.

Silversides

Silversides are small silvery fish that possess scales on the head, large eyes, and two widely separated dorsal fins. Most members of this genus are marine species, but three are found in North American fresh water. One species is found in GSMNP.

BROOK SILVERSIDES
(*Labidesthes sicculus*)

Description. Length to 5 inches. Long, beaklike snout. Two widely separated dorsal fins. Long, sickle-shaped anal fin. Pale green above with silver sides.
Distribution. Near the surface of quiet pools.
Remarks. Completes its full life cycle in one year.

Sunfish

The sunfish family includes the blue gill, crappie, and bass. There are thirty species found in North America. Most have laterally compressed bodies with two dorsal fins—one with spines and one with rays—that appear as one fin. These fish build nests and guard their young.

SMALLMOUTH BASS
(*Micropterus dolomieu*)

Description. Length to 20 inches or more. Dark brown back, often called bronze; yellow-white below. Sides occasionally have several vertical bars or are clear. Red eye. Upper jaw does not extend past rear margin of eye.
Distribution. Clear rivers and lakes with gravel or rocky bottoms.
Remarks. Male actively guards nest.

AMPHIBIANS
AND REPTILES

Amphibian comes from the Greek *amphi,* or "double," and *bios,* which means "life." It refers to the way most frogs, toads, and salamanders begin life in water as a larval form with gills and change over time to a land animal that can breathe air. Amphibians are the only major class of animal that lacks some kind of protective skin covering. Reptiles and fish have scales, birds have feathers, and mammals have fur or hair. Amphibians' skin is thin and moist and thus vulnerable to drying, so they typically inhabit places that are continuously wet or at least damp. Though we may not think of them as such, all adult amphibians are predators. Indeed, they are one of the most numerous and important small predators found in GSMNP. Larger animals such as mountain lions and wolves get the headlines, but the loss of amphibians would likely cause a major collapse of the ecosystem. The number of amphibian species, particularly salamanders, found in GSMNP exceeds that in any other national park.

Reptiles evolved from amphibians some 300 million years ago. There are three major subgroups: turtles, lizards, and snakes. Among the innovations that reptiles developed were strong jaws that can crush insects. The second major development was a shelled egg. This permitted reptiles to sever their ties to water, allowing the colonization of land too arid and too far from water to support amphibians. Reptiles have scaly skin, which is another adaptation that permits them to live on land. Most reptiles breathe through lungs rather than through their skin. Because reptiles rely on outside sources of heat to maintain their internal temperature, it is common to find them basking on rocks or, in some cases, lying on hot pavement. This last behavior puts them at risk from automobiles.

121

Species Accounts

Frogs and Toads

AMERICAN TOAD
(Bufo americanus)

Description. Length to 3.5 inches. Similar to Fowler's toad, but can be distinguished by the presence of only one or two large warts in each of the largest dark spots on the back; chest and abdomen spotted with dark pigment; light mid-dorsal stripe may or may not be present. Color varies tremendously and can be brown, olive, gray, or even yellowish.
Distribution. Found at all elevations in the park, from the lowest to 5,000 feet or more. Sometimes wanders quite far from water.
Remarks. Voice is a sustained musical trill.

FOWLER'S TOAD
(Bufo fowleri)

Description. Length to 3 inches. Typically has three or more warts in each of the largest dark spots on the back. Chest and belly typically unspotted. Color varies from green to brown to gray.
Distribution. Less common than the American toad. More abundant in western portions of the park and generally restricted to lower elevations. Seldom recorded above 3,000 feet.
Remarks. Voice is a short, unmusical bleat that lasts a few seconds.

NORTHERN SPRING PEEPER
(Pseudacris crucifer crucifer)

Description. Length to 1.25 inches. X-shaped cross on the back, on a background of gray, brown, olive, or tan.
Distribution. Found at all elevations in the park. Often associated with brush and trees near water. Wanders farther from water in autumn.
Remarks. The plaintive, shrill notes of this frog can be heard at any season but are most common in late winter and early spring.

EASTERN NARROW-MOUTH TOAD
(Gastrophryne carolinensis)

Description. Length to 1.25 inches. Body rotund, with sharply pointed head and very small mouth. Color varies from brown to green.
Distribution. Very rare in GSMNP. Strongly associated with limestone areas; thus most common in Cades Cove, but also recorded near Townsend just outside the park.
Remarks. Ants are one of its major food preferences.

GREEN FROG
(Rana clamitans melanota)

Description. Length to 3.5 inches. Color varies considerably; can even be more brown than green. Numerous dark spots or blotches on back and sides. Throat of male bright yellow.
Distribution. Well distributed throughout GSMNP along streams and other water sources below 4,000 feet.
Remarks. Voice like a loose banjo string, often repeated three or four times.

PICKEREL FROG
(Rana palustris)

Description. Length to 3 inches. Squarish blotches in parallel rows down back. Bright yellow or orange on inner part of hind legs.
Distribution. Widespread in GSMNP below 3,000 feet.
Remarks. Distasteful skin secretions offer it some protection from predators.

SOUTHERN LEOPARD FROG
(Rana sphenocephala utricularia)

Description. Length to 3.5 inches. A few dark spots on sides. Two or three rows of irregularly placed dark spots between dorsolateral ridges.
Distribution. Not common in GSMNP but ubiquitous in the South. Often found in wet meadows.
Remarks. This the species most often sought for frogs' legs.

WOOD FROG
(Rana sylvatica)

Description. Length to 2.75 inches. Dark "robber's" mask extends back from eye. Color varies tremendously from brown to green.
Distribution. Common at lower elevations in GSMNP. Wanders far from water.
Remarks. On rainy nights during the breeding season in January and February, this species sometimes makes mass migrations, and many are killed by cars.

Salamanders

There are many superlatives that can be claimed for the Smokies, but perhaps the most unknown is the astounding variety of salamanders. Representatives of five of the world's nine families of salamanders are found in GSMNP. Between twenty-one and twenty-nine species (depending on which list you consult) are known to live in the park, although several are rare.

It may be difficult to believe because of their reclusive habits, but the biomass of salamanders in GSMNP exceeds that of all birds and mammals combined. As such, they are major predators in the forest ecosystem, feeding primarily on invertebrates such as insects and earthworms. Some of the aquatic species prey on crayfish, fish, and other amphibians such as frogs.

No generalizations can be made about the life history of these creatures. Some are entirely aquatic. Some have aquatic larvae that become fully terrestrial as adults. Some pass the larval stage in the egg and hatch as complete but miniature versions of the adult. Many salamanders possess toxic skin secretions to discourage predation. Some even bite. Since most salamanders have porous skin, they are extremely vulnerable to air and water pollution. Acid precipitation, in particular, can affect salamander populations.

Salamanders are highly variable in coloration and even skin pattern, making positive identification difficult. The descriptions that follow are, at best, only starting points for identification. Many salamanders are habitat specific. Some are restricted in elevation or even to one side of the park, so attention to location can aid identification.

SPOTTED SALAMANDER
(Ambystoma maculatum)

Description. Length to 9 inches. Color variable from black to dark brown. Belly slate gray. Back has two rows of round, yellow-orange spots, up to fifty in number, running from head to tail.
Distribution. Hardwood forests. Typically found at low elevations in Cades Cove, Elkmont, Laurel Creek, Sugarlands, and the Sinks.
Remarks. Breeds in winter, typically January or February in GSMNP. Sometimes makes mass migrations to breeding areas after warm rains.

MARBLED SALAMANDER
(Ambystoma opacum)

Description. Length to 5 inches. Stocky; black to dark gray above, interrupted by white or silvery gray crossbands. Belly black. Markings are white in males and gray in females.
Distribution. Forest edges. Reported in low-elevation sinkholes in Cades Cove and elsewhere.
Remarks. Banded salamander would be a more descriptive name. Breeds in autumn. Female guards eggs until rain fills nest cavity.

RED SPOTTED NEWT
(Notophthalmus viridescens)

Description. Length to 5 inches. Aquatic and terrestrial forms. Aquatic adult yellowish brown to olive green above, yellow below. Many red spots on back and belly. Terrestrial eft is orange-red.
Distribution. Found on both sides of GSMNP. Prefers small woodland ponds. Has been recorded in Cades Cove, Twentymile Creek, Mingus Creek, and Elkmont, among others.
Remarks. The red eft is sometimes seen after rain. It makes no effort to hide because its skin contains a toxic chemical that discourages predation.

Red spotted newts have a toxin that causes animals that eat them severe discomfort. As a consequence, these newts are active in daylight and easily seen after rains.

MOUNTAIN DUSKY SALAMANDER
(Desmognathus ochrophaeus)

Description. Length to 4 inches. Coloration and pattern vary considerably. Most have a wavy or irregular stripe on the back, with a dark background. Round tail.
Distribution. Very terrestrial. Wanders far from water in wet weather. Typically found under stones and logs near springs and other moist areas.
Remarks. May climb trees when foraging. Also known as the Blue Ridge Mountain salamander.

SANTEETLAH DUSKY SALAMANDER
(Desmognathus santeetlah)

Description. Length to 3.75 inches. Belly washed in yellow. Dorsal color varies, but typically greenish brown with small red spots.
Distribution. Streams, typically above 2,200 feet.
Remarks. Restricted to the Smokies and the Unicoi Mountains on the Tennessee–North Carolina border, plus Great Balsam Mountain of North Carolina.

SEAL SALAMANDER
(Desmognathus monticola)

Description. Length to 5 inches. Stout body; tail compressed and keeled toward the tip. Coloration and markings extremely variable. Black or dark brown markings on light brown or gray background on the dorsal side, with pale below.
Distribution. Ranges from lowlands up to 5,500 feet, where it inhabits cool, moist ravines and streambanks.
Remarks. Said to look like a miniature seal—hence its common name. Ants are a major food item.

SEEPAGE SALAMANDER
(Desmognathus aeneus)

Description. Length to 2.25 inches. Slender. Tail round. Dorsal stripe has a straight-edged reddish brown pattern.
Distribution. Typically found under leaf mold near springs and seepage—hence its common name.
Remarks. A common species in Georgia and Alabama, just reaching into southwestern North Carolina.

SPOTTED DUSKY SALAMANDER
(Desmognathus conanti)

Description. Length to 5.5 inches. Adults have five to eight pairs of round yellow or red spots on the back, sometimes fused to create a stripe. Tail is distinctive, being keeled and triangular in shape with a light line down it.
Distribution. Woodland creeks and seeps.
Remarks. Very similar to the imitator salamander; laboratory analysis is often required to distinguish between the two.

IMITATOR SALAMANDER
(Desmognathus imitator)

Description. Length to 4 inches. Highly variable in color, but usually dark brown. Yellow to red check patches common. Pale line from eye to jaw.
Distribution. Restricted to GSMNP and nearby areas. Found between 4,000 and 5,500 feet in spruce-fir and northern hardwood forests under rocks and logs near seeps and springs.
Remarks. Very similar to the spotted dusky salamander, but prefers higher elevations.

BLACK-BELLIED SALAMANDER
(Desmognathus quadramaculatus)

Description. Length to 6.75 inches. Stout, thick bodied. Tail less than half of total length and knife-edged above. Belly black. Often double row of light dots along flanks.
Distribution. Common along cascading streams and around waterfalls in all the larger streams. In GSMNP, recorded from 1,150 to 6,000 feet.
Remarks. Can swim vigorously if pursued or surprised.

PIGMY SALAMANDER
(Desmognathus wrighti)

Description. Length to 2 inches. One of the smallest salamanders. Tail rounded and less than half the length of the body. Light mid-dorsal stripe, often in a herringbone pattern. Silvery along sides.
Distribution. High-elevation forests, typically above 4,000 feet. Common in spruce-fir forests.
Remarks. Occasionally hunts prey, primarily small insects, in trees.

SHOVELNOSE SALAMANDER
(Desmognathus marmoratus)

Description. Length to 5 inches. Color variable, but generally black, brown, or gray with two rows of blotches or spots along the back. Head wedge shaped and flat.
Distribution. Entirely aquatic and common in most park drainages below 1,500 feet.
Remarks. Hides under stones in mountain streams.

RED-BACKED SALAMANDER
(Plethodon cinereus)

Description. Length to 4 inches. Straight-edged reddish dorsal stripe from head to tail, bordered by dark sides, is the most common color phase. A second variety, known as the lead-backed, is dark gray to black and has been reported in Cades Cove.
Distribution. Woodlands, from low elevations to 5,500 feet.
Remarks. Feeds on earthworms, beetles, and ants.

ZIGZAG SALAMANDER
(Plethodon dorsalis)

Description. Length to 3.75 inches. Light dorsal stripe with lobed borders, typically red or yellow; stripe tends to be very faint in specimens from GSMNP, giving an overall dark cast to the back.
Distribution. Woodland species restricted to elevations below 2,500 feet.
Remarks. Often found hiding under rocks, logs, and other debris.

SLIMY SALAMANDER
(Plethodon glutinosus)

Description. Length to 6.75 inches. Generally black with white flecks on body.
Distribution. Probably the most abundant salamander in GSMNP. Found from 1,200 to 5,500 feet.
Remarks. Skin-gland secretions will stick to your hands if you handle this salamander.

JORDAN'S SALAMANDER
(Plethodon jordani)

Description. Length to 5 inches. Highly variable coloration. Red cheeks and red legs.
Distribution. Woodland species found under forest litter, rotting logs, and rocks at higher elevations, typically above 3,000 feet. Found on Clingmans Dome.
Remarks. Also known as the red-cheeked salamander. Lives in underground burrows, some at least 18 inches long.

FOUR-TOED SALAMANDER
(Hemidactylium scutatum)

Description. Length to 3.5 inches. Four toes (most salamanders have five) on hind feet. Brown above; whitish belly with black spots. Tail constricted near base.
Distribution. Very rare. Associated with sphagnum bogs, which are rare in GSMNP. Recorded in Cades Cove and on Laurel Creek.
Remarks. Adults are terrestrial, and larvae are aquatic.

BLUE RIDGE SPRING SALAMANDER
(Gyrinophilus porphyriticus danielsi)

Description. Length to 7.5 inches. White line from nose to eye, bordered by black or dark brown line. Dorsal colors vary and may be red, salmon, or orange-yellow, with black or brown spots.
Distribution. Found at all elevations near seepage, springs, or mountain streams.
Remarks. Preys on other smaller salamanders.

BLACK-CHINNED RED SALAMANDER
(*Pseudotriton ruber schencki*)

Description. Length to 4.75 inches. Dorsal color reddish pink, with black under chin. Tail spotted.
Distribution. Prefers damp leaves, seeps, and springs. Most abundant below 3,000 feet, but found up to 5,000 feet.
Remarks. Localized to the southern Appalachians in the tristate area of Georgia, North Carolina, and Tennessee.

BLUE RIDGE TWO-LINED SALAMANDER
(*Eurycea bislineata wilderae*)

Description. Length to 4.5 inches. Bright background color. Conspicuous black line from head to tail on both sides of back.
Distribution. Common at all elevations. Typically associated with seeps and springs, but may be found far from water.
Remarks. Has been reported in every month of the year.

JUNALUSKA SALAMANDER
(*Eurycea junaluska*)

Description. Length to 4 inches. Yellowish brown back with black spots on either side, nearly forming a stripe. Tail short, less than half of body length.
Distribution. Generally found below 2,500 feet. Lives under rocks and logs.
Remarks. Very limited range in the Great Smoky Mountains region.

CAVE SALAMANDER
(*Eurycea lucifuga*)

Description. Length to 6 inches. Reddish background (can be yellow to orange-red) with irregularly distributed black spots. Long tail.
Distribution. Strongly associated with limestone caves, although occasionally found outside of them.
Remarks. Sometimes uses its tail to hang on to ledges.

LONG-TAILED SALAMANDER
(*Eurycea longicauda*)

Description. Length to 6 inches. Only yellowish salamander with vertical black marks on a very long, slender tail.
Distribution. Springs, streamsides, and crevices near water. Common at low elevations on the Tennessee side of the mountains, particularly in Cades Cove.
Remarks. Often ventures out to hunt invertebrates on warm, rainy nights.

THREE-LINED SALAMANDER
(*Eurycea longicauda guttolineata*)

Description. Length to 6 inches. Only salamander in GSMNP with three dark stripes, although midline stripe may be broken into a series of dark spots. Background color typically yellow or tan.
Distribution. Associated with seeps and springs. Found only on the North Carolina side of GSMNP. Restricted to elevations below 2,800 feet.
Remarks. Some consider this a subspecies of the long-tailed salamander; other authorities contend that it should be its own distinct species.

Turtles

Six species of turtle have been recorded in GSMNP, including the snapping turtle (*Chelydra serpentina*), eastern spiny soft shell (*Apalone spinifera spinifera*), stripeneck musk turtle (*Sternotherus minor peltifer*), and common map turtle (*Graptemys geographica*). The last three are found only in the lowest reaches of Abrams Creek and are very rare in the park.

EASTERN BOX TURTLE
(*Terrapene carolina carolina*)

Description. Length to 6 inches. High, domelike shell. Exceptionally variable coloration, including yellow, orange, or olive on black or brown.

Distribution. Primarily terrestrial. Found in woodlands from the lowest elevations to about 4,000 feet.

Remarks. In very warm weather, this turtle sometimes lies in mud to cool off.

The box turtle is found in woodlands from the lowest elevations to about 4,000 feet.

EASTERN PAINTED TURTLE
(Chrysemys picta picta)

Description. Length to 6 inches. Rows of scutes on the carapace. Yellow spots on head—two on each side.
Distribution. Aquatic. Found in Cades Cove and in the reservoirs surrounding the park.
Remarks. The lack of ponds and lakes limits the distribution of this turtle in the park.

Lizards

Lizards are similar to snakes and probably represent a more primitive version of them. Lizards look something like salamanders, but they have several adaptations that permit them to live on land. They have scaly skin, lungs so they can breathe air, and sharp claws that allow them to climb trees and cling to the surfaces of rocks.

NORTHERN FENCE LIZARD
(Sceloporus undulatus hyacinthinus)

Description. Length to 7 inches. Gray-brown body with dark line running down the thigh. Sexes have different markings. Males are typically brown and marked on the undersides, with a bluish throat area often surrounded by black. Females are gray and have wavy markings on their backs, with a smaller amount of blue in the throat area.
Distribution. Common in oak and pine forests at low and mid elevations.
Remarks. These lizards are sometimes active on warm winter days.

NORTHERN GREEN ANOLE
(Anolis carolinensis carolinensis)

Description. Length to 8 inches. Green color and a pink throat fan distinguish this species from other lizards.
Distribution. This southern species reaches its northern limit in GSMNP and is found only below 1,800 feet, primarily in the western sections of the park.
Remarks. Also known as a chameleon.

FIVE-LINED SKINK
(Eumeces fasciatus)

Description. Length to 8.5 inches. Highly variable markings and coloration, depending on age and sex. Young have blue tails that fade with age. Adult males have five faint lines on the back, with a gray tail and reddish face. Females retain the stripe pattern more clearly.
Distribution. Most common skink in GSMNP. Abundant below 2,500 feet, but found up to 5,000 feet or more. Likes old boards, rock, logs, and other cover.
Remarks. Occasionally climbs trees and shrubs looking for insects.

SOUTHEASTERN FIVE-LINED SKINK
Eumeces inexpectatus)

Description. Length to 8.5 inches. Brown or black with five narrow stripes that fade with maturity. Tail blue or gray. Breeding male has reddish head.
Distribution. Tolerates drier habitat than other skinks; sometimes associated with oak forests and open pine woodlands.
Remarks. Climbs well.

BROADHEAD SKINK
(*Eumeces laticeps*)

Description. Length to 12.75 inches. Very large and robust compared with other skinks. Males tend to be olive-brown with orange-red heads. Females similar to five-lined skink.
Distribution. Found mostly below 2,000 feet. Not very common.
Remarks. The most arboreal of lizards; frequently found in hollow trees.

SIX-LINED RACE RUNNER
(*Cnemidophorus sexlineatus sexlineatus*)

Description. Length to 10.5 inches. Has six to seven light stripes separated by dark bands. Throat green to blue in males, white in females. Tail brown but striped on sides.
Distribution. Uncommon in GSMNP. Prefers dry, open terrain below 2,000 feet. Has been observed near Abrams Creek, along the shore of Fontana Reservoir, and at Sugarlands.
Remarks. Fast-moving lizard.

Snakes

Snakes are essentially legless lizards. Snakes also lack external ear openings, and they have transparent scales that cover their eyes. The skull bones of many snakes can be stretched, allowing them to swallow large prey whole. Most snakes are harmless; in GSMNP, only the copperhead and rattlesnake are poisonous.

EASTERN WORM SNAKE
(*Carphophis amoenus amoenus*)

Description. Length to 11 inches. Looks like an earthworm. Plain brown. Head pointed.
Distribution. Common in GSMNP on both sides of the mountains. Typically found under stones or logs.
Remarks. Hides underground in burrows in dry weather.

NORTHERN BLACK RACER
(*Coluber constrictor constrictor*)

Description. Length to 60 inches. Slender black snake, sometimes with white on chin or throat.
Distribution. Common in GSMNP in old fields, but also found in woodlands up to 4,600 feet.
Remarks. Very fast snake that tends to retreat upward into bushes or branches if pursued or frightened.

NORTHERN RINGNECK SNAKE
(*Diadophis punctatus edwardsii*)

Description. Length to 15 inches. Dark, slender, with golden collar. Dorsal color variable. Belly yellow.
Distribution. Fairly common. Found from 1,000 feet up to 5,800 feet on Andrews Bald.
Remarks. Secretive and seldom seen, despite its abundance.

CORN SNAKE
(Elaphe guttata guttata)

Description. Length to 48 inches. Typically red or orange above, but can be brown or gray with bold black and white pattern on belly. Dorsal reddish brown spots or blotches outlined in black.
Distribution. Rocky hillsides, woodlands, and pine forests. Generally found below 2,500 feet. Recorded at Elkmont, park headquarters, Abrams Creek, Townsend, and Sugarlands.
Remarks. Climbs trees and shrubs well.

BLACK RAT SNAKE
(Elaphe obsoleta obsoleta)

Description. Length to 72 inches. Usually plain black, but occasionally displays slight spotted pattern. Chin and throat white or cream.
Distribution. Common in GSMNP up to 4,400 feet.
Remarks. Exceptional climber; sometimes dens in hollow trees.

EASTERN HOGNOSE SNAKE
(Heterodon platirhinos)

Description. Length to 33 inches. Upturned snout. Color variable; can be brown, red, gray, yellow, or olive. Typically has spots.
Distribution. Uncommon in GSMNP. Found in open habitat below 2,500 feet. Found at Cosby, Elkmont, Sugarlands, Cades Cove, and Cherokee.
Remarks. This snake hisses loudly when disturbed. If that doesn't work, it plays possum by flipping over on its back and remaining still with its jaws open.

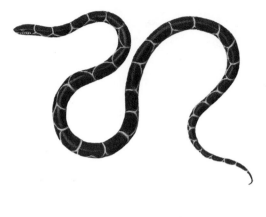

COMMON KING SNAKE
(*Lampropeltis getula*)

Description. Length to 48 inches. Black with white or cream lines encircling the body, forming "chain links."
Distribution. Two subspecies in the park—eastern king snake (*Lampropeltis getula getula*) on the North Carolina side, and black king snake (*Lampropeltis getula nigra*) on the Tennessee side. Specimens recorded in Deep Creek, Smokemont, Cades Cove, and Sugarlands.
Remarks. Eats other snakes, including copperheads and rattlesnakes.

NORTHERN WATER SNAKE
(*Nerodia sipedon sipedon*)

Description. Length to 42 inches. Dark dorsal markings are bands near the head, becoming more like blotches near the tail. Pattern is obscure in adults, resulting in a brown or nearly black snake.
Distribution. One of the most common snakes in GSMNP. Found in nearly all watersheds below 3,000 feet, though occasionally found higher.
Remarks. Eats fish, tadpoles, and other aquatic life.

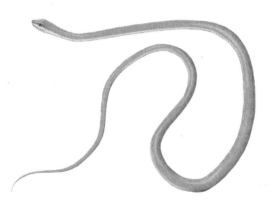

ROUGH GREEN SNAKE
(*Opheodrys aestivus*)

Description. Length to 32 inches. Slender. Light green above; white, yellow, or light green below.
Distribution. Generally found below 3,000 feet and associated with dense shrubs along waterways.
Remarks. An excellent climber and swimmer. Sometimes called "vine" snake because of its resemblance to a vine when motionless.

NORTHERN BROWN SNAKE
(Storeria dekayi dekayi)

Description. Length to 13 inches. Can be a variety of colors, though brown is most common. Parallel rows of black spots down back, often connected by dark cross-lines.
Distribution. Uncommon. Has been found along Abrams Creek and at Sugarlands.
Remarks. Secretive and not often seen.

NORTHERN REDBELLY SNAKE
(Storeria occipitomaculata)

Description. Length to 10 inches. Color varies from gray to black. Similar to northern brown snake, but has pure red belly and pale-colored nape spot.
Distribution. Uncommon in GSMNP. Frequents open woods in uplands. Reported in Newfound Gap, Spruce Mountain, Alum Cave Bluff, Abrams Creek, Tremont, Laurel Creek, Cades Cove, and Flat Creek.
Remarks. Curls up its lip when startled.

EASTERN GARTER SNAKE
(Thamnophis sirtalis sirtalis)

Description. Length to 26 inches. Extremely variable in color and pattern. Lateral stripes confined to rows two and three. Typically has three yellow stripes, but they can be green, blue, or brown. Background color can be brown, green, olive, or black. Many garter snakes found at higher elevations in GSMNP tend to be dark.
Distribution. Found throughout the park.
Remarks. Bears live young.

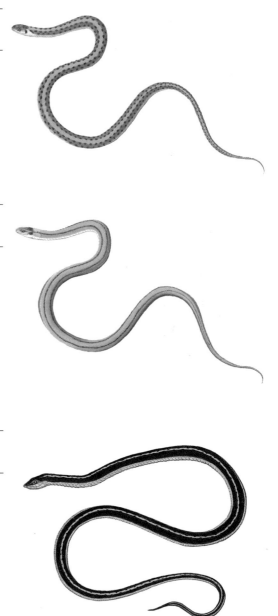

NORTHERN COPPERHEAD
(Agkistrodon contortrix mokasen)

Description. Length to 36 inches. Coppery red head with an hourglass pattern. Chestnut crossbands are wide on the sides and narrow at the top of the back.
Distribution. Prefers rocky terrain. In GSMNP, usually below 2,500 feet.
Remarks. Vibrates its tail if agitated, often causing leaves to rattle. Large groups of copperheads gather in autumn when preparing to enter their winter den. They eat mice and other rodents but also enjoy locusts.

TIMBER RATTLESNAKE
(Crotalus horridus)

Description. Length to 60 inches. Black or dark brown crossbands on a pale gray, yellowish, or tan background.
Distribution. Common and widespread in all major watersheds in GSMNP up to 6,600 feet. Though found in the spruce-fir zone, they are rare in this forest type. Found on balds such as Gregory Bald and Andrews Bald.
Remarks. A food study revealed that rodents and other small mammals make up the bulk of their diet, but an occasional bird is eaten.

Birds

Great Smoky Mountains National Park stands as a green, leafy island in the midst of a largely fragmented and developed landscape. As such, it is particularly valuable to bird species that depend on old-growth forests and undisturbed habitats. More than 230 bird species have been recorded within the park borders, and 110 are known to breed in the park.

The park's elevational range—spanning more than 5,000 vertical feet—ensures a multitude of different climates and habitats. Many bird species are stratified by elevation and habitat. For instance, birds most common at the lowest elevations in the southern hardwood forest include the Acadian flycatcher, blue-gray gnatcatcher, red-bellied woodpecker, belted kingfisher, downy woodpecker, wood thrush, hooded warbler, blue jay, Carolina chickadee, Carolina wren, eastern bluebird, scarlet tanager, yellow-throated warbler, and ovenbird.

As one ascends higher into the northern hardwood and cove forests of the middle elevations, the bird species change somewhat. Many of the same species found at lower elevations reach their upper limits in this zone, while birds more typical of northern locations may reach their lower limits. These include the veery, yellow-bellied sapsucker, black-throated blue warbler, dark-eyed junco, solitary vireo, and tufted titmouse.

At the highest elevations are the spruce-fir forests, which are more typical of Canada and northern New England. A number of species reach their southern limits in GSMNP, including several "boreal" species that nest or reside in the spruce-fir forests that crown the park's mountaintops. Included in this group are the winter wren, Canada warbler, veery, black-burnian warbler, black-capped chickadee, northern saw-whet owl, red-breasted nuthatch, and golden-crowned kinglet.

Although not particularly common in GSMNP, the open landscape of Cades Cove provides specialized habitat for birds more typical of open woodlands or meadow habitats. These include the red-tailed hawk, wild turkey, American robin, eastern meadowlark, eastern kingbird, barn swallow, kestrel, and American crow.

Of the more than 230 species recorded in GSMNP, only 60 or so are year-round residents. Some birds seen frequently in the park are only seasonal residents or merely passing through. For instance, many hawk species are common during the autumn migration but are seldom seen at other times of the year.

A guide to all the birds found in GSMNP would be a volume in itself. The following list is limited to birds that are known residents in the park or are particularly abundant. Migrants, birds seen only rarely, or those with only a few recorded sightings are not included.

Species Accounts

Vultures

Vultures are hawklike soaring birds that feed on carrion. They use scent to locate food. Their naked heads prevent matted blood from accumulating while feeding.

TURKEY VULTURE
(*Cathartes aura*)

Description. Naked red head. Body black except for silver-gray wings. Often glides with wings held in a V shape.
Distribution. Common resident in open country such as Cades Cove.
Remarks. Has been known to nest in GSMNP and at "Buzzard Rocks" (named for them) near Chilhowee Mountain.

Hawks and Falcons

These birds of prey capture rodents and other birds—often on the wing. There are four major groups: eagles and ospreys, with large wings and broad tails; buteos, which have broad wings and wide tails and soar; accipiters, with broad wings and long tails, which flap their wings more than soar; and falcons, which have long tails and pointed wings made for speed. There are fifteen species occasionally reported in GSMNP, particularly during migrations, but only six breed there.

COOPER'S HAWK
(Accipiter cooperii)

Description. Length to 20 inches. Rounded wings, longish round tail, reddish barred chest, grayish back.
Distribution. Uncommon. Typically found in riverside woodlands. Most frequently seen during September–October migration.
Remarks. Hunts birds and small mammals in the forest, often capturing other birds on the wing.

SHARP-SHINNED HAWK
(Accipiter striatus)

Description. Length to 14 inches. Similar in appearance to Cooper's hawk. Has rounded wings but a slightly shorter, squarish tail.
Distribution. Uncommon. Most abundant in woodlands and forest.
Remarks. Preys largely on small birds caught on the wing.

RED-TAILED HAWK
(Buteo jamaicensis)

Description. Length to 22 inches. Broad wings and tail. Often light colored beneath, with dark mantle around head and forward part of wings. Distinctive reddish tail.
Distribution. Hawks in general are not common here. They are most often associated with open meadows and woodlands; primarily seen in Cades Cove.
Remarks. Often seen soaring. The most common hawk in GSMNP.

RED-SHOULDERED HAWK
(Buteo lineatus)

Description. Length to 19 inches. Broad wings and tail. Reddish shoulders and wing linings. Tends to fly with several short wing beats followed by a glide.
Distribution. Occasional resident. Found in woodlands, particularly near water.
Remarks. A bird of mature forests at low elevations.

BROAD-WINGED HAWK
(Buteo platypterus)

Description. Length to 16 inches. Broad wings and tail. White chest, belly, and underwings. Tail has white and black bands.
Distribution. Rather common in hardwood forests.
Remarks. The best time to see this bird is during fall migration.

AMERICAN KESTREL
(Falco sparverius)

Description. Length to 11 inches. Smallish falcon with pointed wings and long, narrow tail. Reddish back and black stripes on face.
Distribution. Uncommon. Typically seen in open country such as Cades Cove and Oconaluftee.
Remarks. Nests in tree cavities. Often seen hovering over fields.

Grouse and Turkey

All these birds are chickenlike and typically walk rather than fly.

WILD TURKEY
(Meleagris gallopavo)

Description. Length to 45 inches. Iridescent body. Red wattles in male. Bare-skinned head.
Distribution. Uncommon resident. Seen in open woodlands and the edges of fields such as Cades Cove.
Remarks. The largest bird in the park. In spring, gobbling by males can be heard up to a mile away.

RUFFED GROUSE
(Bonasa umbellus)

Description. Length to 17 inches. Brownish chickenlike bird. Black ruff on side of neck. Dark band on tip of tail.
Distribution. Fairly common in woodlands at all elevations.
Remarks. Male "drums" on hollow logs in spring to attract females.

Shorebirds

As their name implies, these birds are common along shorelines, usually the ocean, but occasionally inland streams and lakes. They tend to have plump, compact bodies. At least fourteen species have been recorded in the park during migration, but only two are regular residents.

KILLDEER
(Charadrius vociferus)

Description. Length 10 inches. Brown back and white belly, chest, and throat, with two black bands across upper chest.
Distribution. Uncommon resident found in open terrain such as Cades Cove.
Remarks. The killdeer "fakes" a broken wing to lure predators from the nest.

AMERICAN WOODCOCK
(Scolopax minor)

Description. Length 11 inches. Long bill with chunky body, almost no tail.
Distribution. Uncommon resident. Found at all elevations, but secretive. Prefers moist woodlands and open, grassy fields. May nest on grassy balds.
Remarks. Courtship display involves elaborate flight—circling high and spiraling back to earth.

Doves

These pigeonlike birds are strong and fast fliers.

MOURNING DOVE
(*Zenaida macroura*)

Description. Length 12 inches. Light tannish brown on back, paler pink on chest and belly. Long, pointed tail.
Distribution. Common resident. Prefers open country such as Cades Cove and Oconaluftee, typically below 2,000 feet.
Remarks. One of the earliest birds to nest in the park. Voice is a low cooing sound.

Cuckoos

Cuckoos are long-tailed birds.

BLACK-BILLED CUCKOO
(*Coccyzus erythropthalmus*)

Description. Length 12 inches. Brown-gray above and pale gray-white below. Long tail patterned gray and white on underside.
Distribution. Uncommon summer visitor. Found along woodland streams at higher elevations—typically above 3,500 feet.
Remarks. This northern bird reaches its southern limit in the vicinity of GSMNP.

Owls

Owls are nighttime birds of prey with immobile eyes set in large heads.

EASTERN SCREECH-OWL
(*Otus asio*)

Description. Length 8 inches. Yellow eyes; prominent ear tufts. Color varies from reddish to gray.
Distribution. Fairly common resident in woodlands below 4,500 feet.
Remarks. Roosts in tree cavities. Song is a quavering whistle rather than a screech. Eats quite a few insects, as well as small rodents.

GREAT HORNED OWL
(*Bubo virginianus*)

Description. Length 22 inches. Large brownish owl with obvious ear tufts. White throat.
Distribution. Uncommon resident in mature deciduous forests and edges of fields below 4,500 feet (usually lower).
Remarks. Call is a series of three to eight hoots.

BARRED OWL
(Strix varia)

Description. Length 21 inches. Chunky brown owl with dark barring on chest. Lacks "horned" ear tufts.
Distribution. Fairly common resident at all elevations, including spruce-fir forests on Clingmans Dome, Newfound Gap, and lower elevations such as Cades Cove.
Remarks. Call sounds like "who cooks for you."

NORTHERN SAW-WHET OWL
(Aegolius acadicus)

Description. Length 8 inches. Tiny reddish brown body with white streaks on chest.
Distribution. Fairly common resident at higher elevations, mostly above 4,500 feet. Most often seen in spruce-fir zone at Newfound Gap and along the road to Clingmans Dome.
Remarks. Voice is a monotone, likened to the sound of a saw being sharpened.

Nightjars

Nightjars use their wide mouths to snag insects on the wing. They are most often seen in the evening. Three species have been reported in the park, but only one is resident.

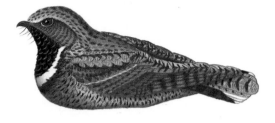

WHIP-POOR-WILL
(*Caprimulgus vociferus*)

Description. Length 10 inches. Mottled brown on back. Tips of wings and tail rounded.
Distribution. Fairly common summer resident below 3,000 feet. Often heard calling at Smokemont, Cades Cove, and Cosby.
Remarks. Call a loud *whip-poor-will.*

Hummingbirds

These tiny birds have long, needlelike bills for sipping flower nectar. Their ability to hover in flight is distinctive. Only one species is found in the eastern United States.

RUBY-THROATED HUMMINGBIRD
(*Archilochus colubris*)

Description. Length under 4 inches. Metallic green above, with ruby throat patch in males; females have white throat patch.
Distribution. Fairly common summer resident at all elevations.
Remarks. Hummingbirds go into torpor at night to save energy.

Kingfishers

Kingfishers hover over water looking for prey and plunge in headfirst to capture small fish.

BELTED KINGFISHER
(Ceryle alcyon)

Description. Length 13 inches. Grayish blue back and head, with gray-blue breast band. Large head with ragged crest; stout bill; short legs.
Distribution. Fairly common resident along streams below 3,000 feet, particularly the Pigeon and Little Rivers.
Remarks. Digs burrows in mud banks. Loud, rattling call.

Woodpeckers

Woodpeckers are tree climbers with sharp claws, stiff tail feathers, and a sharp bill for excavating insects from tree bark. Eight species have been recorded in the park.

NORTHERN FLICKER
(Colaptes auratus)

Description. Length 12 inches. Brown, barred back; black dots on light chest and belly. Red crescent on neck.
Distribution. Fairly common resident at nearly all elevations except for the highest spruce-fir zone, but does nest on the edges of balds.
Remarks. Spends a lot of time on the ground feeding on ants.

RED-HEADED WOODPECKER
(Melanerpes erythrocephalus)

Description. Length 9 inches. Head bright red. White chest and belly. Back and tail black, with white rump and inner wing feathers.
Distribution. Uncommon resident in woodlands and open areas, typically below 3,500 feet, except during migration.
Remarks. Once far more common in the park, but declining in part due to competition for cavities with European starling.

RED-BELLIED WOODPECKER
(Melanerpes carolinus)

Description. Length 9 inches. Back barred black and white. Back of head bright red. Pale reddish belly with otherwise light underparts.
Distribution. Fairly common resident in lower-elevation woodlands, including the area near Sugarlands and Metcalf Bottoms.
Remarks. The reddish belly patch is sometimes difficult to spot.

YELLOW-BELLIED SAPSUCKER
(Sphyrapicus varius)

Description. Length 8 inches. Black and white striping on head, with red fore-crown. Black bib and yellowish belly.
Distribution. Uncommon summer resident, typically in hardwoods above 3,500 feet.
Remarks. Sapsuckers drill holes in trees and return later to capture insects attracted to the juice.

Rectangular holes 2 to 4 inches in size are made by pileated woodpeckers. The black, white, and red bird is the largest woodpecker in GSMNP.

PILEATED WOODPECKER
(Dryocopus pileatus)

Description. Length 16 inches. Mostly black with red crest and black and white striping on face and neck. Large white wing patches obvious during flight.
Distribution. Fairly common resident in older mature forests.
Remarks. This is the largest woodpecker in North America. It makes a distinctive, loud drumming noise as it chisels holes.

DOWNY WOODPECKER
(Picoides pubescens)

Description. Length 7 inches. White back, white spots on wings against black background, small red crown, white underparts. Small bill distinguishes it from the similar and slightly larger hairy woodpecker.
Distribution. Fairly common resident, chiefly found below 3,500 feet.
Remarks. One of the most common woodpeckers seen at bird feeders.

HAIRY WOODPECKER
(Picoides villosus)

Description. Length to 9 inches. Slightly larger version of the downy woodpecker. Stouter bill; outer tail feathers all white.
Distribution. Fairly common resident, though more likely to be seen at higher elevations than the downy woodpecker. The most common woodpecker in the spruce-fir zone.
Remarks. Drums on a tree with its bill to attract a mate and establish territory.

Flycatchers

Flycatchers launch themselves from perches in trees to capture flying insects. The species are often very difficult to tell apart. Twelve species have been reported in GSMNP, but only seven breed there.

OLIVE-SIDED FLYCATCHER
(Contopus cooperi)

Description. Length 7 inches. Dark olive-brown back and head, with white spots near rump. Throat and belly white.
Distribution. Uncommon summer resident in the spruce-fir zone. Can often be seen near Newfound Gap.
Remarks. This boreal species reaches its southern limit in GSMNP. Often seen perching on dead snags or branches.

ACADIAN FLYCATCHER
(Empidonax virescens)

Description. Length 6 inches. Olive green back, tail, neck, and head. Whitish wing bars against dark brown wings. Yellow eye ring. Yellowish belly and white lower breast.
Distribution. Common summer resident in shrubs and forests along streams and ravines below 3,500 feet. Particularly common among rhododendrons.
Remarks. *Empidonax* species are very difficult to tell apart. Most birders rely on voice to distinguish them.

EASTERN KINGBIRD
(Tyrannus tyrannus)

Description. Length 8 inches. Black head, back, and tail. White throat, chest, and belly.
Distribution. Fairly common summer resident of open areas such as Cades Cove.
Remarks. Sits on a conspicuous perch such as a fence post, occasionally darting forth to capture flying insects, which are its chief food.

EASTERN PHOEBE
(Sayornis phoebe)

Description. Length 7 inches. Gray-brown above, with light undersides. Pale gray band across chest. No wing bars.
Distribution. Common resident, mostly below 3,000 feet.
Remarks. Only flycatcher that remains year-round in the park. Often nests around buildings and bridges.

Vireos

Vireos are small songbirds with short, slightly hooked bills. They resemble warblers but are less active. Six species have been recorded in the park, but only four breed there.

WHITE-EYED VIREO
(Vireo griseus)

Description. Length 5 inches. Gray-olive above, with yellowish sides and chest. White belly and throat.
Distribution. Fairly common summer resident below 3,000 feet in thickets and fields such as those bordering Cades Cove.
Remarks. Boldly defends nests against intruders.

BLUE-HEADED VIREO
(Vireo solitarius)

Description. Length 5 inches. Bluish head fading to olive-brown on back. Yellowish sides fading to white on belly and throat.
Distribution. Common summer resident from 2,000 feet upward, and the only vireo typically found in the spruce-fir forest.
Remarks. Previously called the solitary vireo.

RED-EYED VIREO
(Vireo olivaceus)

Description. Length 6 inches. Prominent eye strip and red eye. Greenish back with gray-blue crown. White underparts.
Distribution. Abundant summer resident below 4,000 feet.
Remarks. Males sing almost continuously from treetops.

Jays and Crows

These loud and aggressive birds are highly adaptable to many different environments.

COMMON RAVEN
(*Corvus corax*)

Description. Length 24 inches. Completely black with thicker, stouter bill than the crow. Wedge-shaped tail obvious when flying. Voice a croak.
Distribution. Fairly common resident, especially at higher elevations. Frequently seen soaring above the spruce-fir zone in places such as Clingmans Dome.
Remarks. Largest of the songbirds. Ravenfork in the park is named for this species.

BLUE JAY
(*Cyanocitta cristata*)

Description. Length 11 inches. Blue crest, back, wings, and tail. White and black barring on wings, white underparts. Raucous *jay, jay, jay* call.
Distribution. Common resident throughout the park.
Remarks. Often feeds on acorns. The extras cached in the soil frequently sprout new trees.

Swallows

Swallows have long, pointed wings and slender bodies. They are often seen darting about catching insects on the wing. Six species have been recorded in the park, but only two breed there.

BARN SWALLOW
(Hirundo rustica)

Description. Length 7 inches. Distinctive deeply forked tail. Throat reddish brown; underparts rust to cinnamon.
Distribution. Common summer resident in open fields, typically at the lowest elevations in the park, including the Oconaluftee and Cades Cove areas.
Remarks. Sometimes nests in small colonies, often in barns—hence its name.

Chickadees and Titmice

These small, active birds have short wings and short bills.

TUFTED TITMOUSE
(Baeolophus bicolor)

Description. Length 7 inches. Grayish back, tail, and head with gray crest. Underparts pale with pale brown flank.
Distribution. Fairly common resident in deciduous forests below 5,000 feet.
Remarks. Often forages in small, mixed-species flocks with chickadees and nuthatches.

CAROLINA CHICKADEE
(Poecile carolinensis)

Description. Length 5 inches. Very similar to black-capped chickadee, with black bib and cap, grayish back, white underparts. Best distinguished by call, which is faster than the black-capped chickadee's.
Distribution. Common resident of lower and middle elevations below 4,000 feet.
Remarks. These active, inquisitive birds often investigate squeaking sounds.

BLACK-CAPPED CHICKADEE
(Poecile atricapillus)

Description. Length 5 inches. Black bib and cap, grayish back, pale undersides.
Distribution. Fairly common resident above 4,000 feet in summer breeding season, moving to lower elevations in winter.
Remarks. Most chickadees seen in spruce-fir forests are the black-capped variety.

Nuthatches and Creepers

These small tree climbers move up and down trees searching for insects in the bark.

WHITE-BREASTED NUTHATCH
(Sitta carolinensis)

Description. Length 6 inches. Small, pointed bill. Black cap and grayish back. White face, throat, and underparts.
Distribution. Fairly common resident in deciduous forests from lowlands to just below the spruce-fir zone.
Remarks. Lives in cavities that it excavates itself.

RED-BREASTED NUTHATCH
(*Sitta canadensis*)

Description. Length 5 inches. Black cap and eye stripe, with white line above eye. Grayish back and tail. Rusty throat, chest, and belly.
Distribution. Common resident in the spruce-fir forest.
Remarks. Call sounds like a tin horn.

BROWN CREEPER
(*Certhia americana*)

Description. Length 5 inches. Streaked brown, with stiff tail. When feeding, spirals upward from base of tree, then flies to next tree and starts again at the bottom.
Distribution. Fairly common resident above 4,500 feet. Most often associated with the spruce-fir forest in summer, but moves to lower elevations in winter.
Remarks. The nest is constructed under a loose slab of bark.

Wrens

Wrens are small, chunky birds with slender bills. Their tails rise at a perky, uplifted angle. Six species have been recorded in the park.

WINTER WREN
(*Troglodytes troglodytes*)

Description. Length 4 inches. Stubby tail held at perked angle. Generally dark brown back, neck, and tail. Grayish throat and chest. Dark bars on belly.
Distribution. Fairly common resident of higher spruce-fir zone. Winters at lower elevations.
Remarks. Very beautiful musical song.

Kinglets

Kinglets are small birds that jump from branch to branch and flit about. Two species have been recorded in the park, but only one is common.

GOLDEN-CROWNED KINGLET
(*Regulus satrapa*)

Description. Length 4 inches. Male has orangish crown patch lined by black and white stripes. Female has yellow crown. Underparts whitish gray; back, neck, and tail olive green. White wing bars.
Distribution. Common resident of spruce-fir forests. Easily seen along Clingmans Dome Road.
Remarks. The golden-crowned is the only resident kinglet in the park, but the closely related ruby-crowned kinglet is seen at lower elevations in winter and during migration.

Thrushes

Well known for their songs, thrushes are found in a variety of habitats. Seven species have been recorded in the park, but only four are common.

EASTERN BLUEBIRD
(*Sialia sialis*)

Description. Length to 7 inches. Male deep blue above with reddish throat and chest, white belly. Female gray-blue above with chestnut throat and chest, white belly.
Distribution. Fairly common resident below 5,000 feet. Typically found in open areas such as Cades Cove and Oconaluftee.
Remarks. Nests in tree cavities.

VEERY
(Catharus fuscescens)

Description. Length 7 inches. Reddish brown above, with white underparts. Spotted breast.
Distribution. Common summer resident above 3,500 feet in the northern hardwood and spruce-fir zones. Spends a lot of time on the forest floor foraging.
Remarks. Has a beautiful, cascading, flutelike song.

WOOD THRUSH
(Hylocicha mustelina)

Description. Length 8 inches. Reddish brown above; white below, with heavily spotted breast and belly. White eye ring.
Distribution. Common summer resident in deciduous forests below 5,000 feet, where it spends a lot of time on the forest floor. Easily seen (and heard) around Sugarlands, Cosby, and Cades Cove.
Remarks. Beautiful flutelike song. The veery and the wood thrush overlap somewhat in middle elevations, but the wood thrush is more common in lower-elevation woodlands, and the veery is more common in higher forests.

AMERICAN ROBIN
(Turdus migratorius)

Description. Length 10 inches. Brown above with dark tail; reddish throat, breast, and belly.
Distribution. Fairly common resident throughout the park. Found in all habitats from lowland open meadows to spruce-fir forests.
Remarks. Lovely song is *cheerily cheerily cheer-up*.

Thrashers

These medium-size birds have a rich repertoire of songs. Three thrashers have been reported in the park, but only two are common.

GRAY CATBIRD
(Dumetella carolinensis)

Description. Length 8 inches. Gray with black cap. Long black tail with chestnut red undertail.
Distribution. Fairly common summer resident found throughout the park, but most abundant at lower elevations. Prefers dense tangles, thickets, and undergrowth of blackberry and rhododendron or near downed trees.
Remarks. Call is a catlike mew—hence its name.

Starlings

These chunky, dark birds have iridescent feathers.

EUROPEAN STARLING
(Sturnus vulgaris)

Description. Length 8 inches. Yellow bill, iridescent blue-black body.
Distribution. Common resident around human habitation, including Cades Cove, Elkmont, and Oconaluftee.
Remarks. Introduced from Europe and now widely distributed across the United States.

Waxwings

Waxwings have yellow-tipped tails and pointed crests. They often form foraging flocks.

CEDAR WAXWING
(Bombycilla cedrorum)

Description. Length 7 inches. Brown crest, neck, and back. Grayish rump. Black tail with yellow tip. Belly yellowish.
Distribution. Fairly common resident found at all elevations. More common at high elevations in summer and low elevations in winter.
Remarks. Seeks out berries and fruits, so is erratic in its wanderings.

Warblers

Warblers are small, flighty birds that flit from branch to branch. Thirty-eight species have been recorded in the park. Warblers divide up the landscape, with different species foraging in habitats ranging from willow shrubs to spruce-fir forests. Sometimes they even divvy up the same habitat, with some species focusing on the treetops and others feeding on lower branches.

NORTHERN PARULA
(Parula americana)

Description. Length 4 inches. Gray-blue above, with yellowish back patch. White belly, yellow chest and throat. White wing bars.
Distribution. Fairly common summer resident below 5,000 feet, frequently in woodlands along streams and wet areas, such as Gum Swamp near Cades Cove.
Remarks. Smallest warbler in the park.

YELLOW WARBLER
(Dendroica petechia)

Description. Length 5 inches. Yellow overall, with yellowish olive back. Male has red-streaked breast.

Distribution. Fairly common summer resident below 3,000 feet. Prefers open, shrubby areas such as streamside willow patches.

Remarks. Migrates south earlier than most birds, leaving the park by August.

CHESTNUT-SIDED WARBLER
(Dendroica pensylvanica)

Description. Length 5 inches. Breeding males have yellow crown, black eye line, and chestnut on side. Females have greenish crown and less chestnut.

Distribution. Common summer resident above 3,000 feet in brushy, disturbed sites, such as along the margins of balds and in rhododendron and blackberry patches.

Remarks. Breeding activity peaks in mid-June.

BLACK-THROATED GREEN WARBLER
(Dendroica virens)

Description. Length 5 inches. Green upperparts, greenish ear patch, yellow face. Male has black throat and upper breast. Female has less black.

Distribution. Common summer resident in forests at all elevations.

Remarks. Most widespread warbler in the park.

YELLOW-RUMPED WARBLER
(Dendroica coronata)

Description. Length 5 inches. Yellow rump, yellow patch on sides, yellow crown patch, white throat and belly. Otherwise, black to gray, with black bib and eye patch in males, streaked black bib in females.
Distribution. Abundant in open areas along streams and in brushy areas.
Remarks. Only warbler likely to be seen in winter.

BLACKBURNIAN WARBLER
(Dendroica fusca)

Description. Length 5 inches. Male has bright orange throat; white wing patch; black back, neck, crown, and ear patch. Female has paler throat and double wing bar.
Distribution. Fairly common summer resident above 3,000 feet, particularly among the spruce-fir forests. Easily seen along Clingmans Dome Road.
Remarks. Forages and sings high in treetops.

PINE WARBLER
(Dendroica pinus)

Description. Length 5 inches. Drab brown above, with yellowish underparts; white under tail. Female duller. Longish bill.
Distribution. Fairly common migrant and less common summer resident at lower elevations among pines.
Remarks. Pine warblers sing in the spring, remain silent through the summer, then begin singing again in September.

BLACK-AND-WHITE WARBLER
(*Mniotilta varia*)

Description. Length 5 inches. Black and white streaking on back and sides, with white belly. Male has black throat; female has white throat, breast, and belly.
Distribution. Common summer resident below 5,000 feet in forests.
Remarks. Works its way up and down trees like a nuthatch.

AMERICAN REDSTART
(*Setophaga ruticilla*)

Description. Length 5 inches. Male black overall, white belly, orange wing patch, orange along tail near rump. Female grayish green above and white below, with yellow patches along tail near rump.
Distribution. Fairly common summer resident in disturbed edge habitat and second-growth forests below 2,500 feet. Look for it along Little River Road and near Sugarlands.
Remarks. Sometimes acts like flycatcher, capturing insects in midair.

WORM-EATING WARBLER
(*Helmitheros vermivorus*)

Description. Length 5 inches. Brown-green above, with buffy chest and dull brown belly. Black stripes on buffy head.
Distribution. Fairly common summer resident on forested hillsides below 3,000 feet. Laurel Falls and Gregory Ridge Trails are good places to see them.
Remarks. Spends a lot of time on the forest floor foraging.

OVENBIRD
(Seiurus aurocapillus)

Description. Length 6 inches. Brown above, with russet-orange crown bordered by black stripes. Breast white with black streaks. Pink legs.
Distribution. Common summer resident in mature forests below 5,000 feet.
Remarks. Often forages on the ground like a thrush.

LOUISIANA WATERTHRUSH
(Seiurus motacilla)

Description. Length 6 inches. Dark above, with dark streaking on light breast. White eye stripe.
Distribution. Common summer resident along streams below 3,500 feet. Can often be observed near Sugarlands and along Little River.
Remarks. Walks rather than hops on the forest floor.

KENTUCKY WARBLER
(Oporornis formosus)

Description. Length 5 inches. Olive brown above, with bright yellow undersides. Yellow eye patch. Black crown and cheek patch. Long legged.
Distribution. Common summer resident in deciduous woodlands below 3,500 feet, particularly in ravines and along streams.
Remarks. Nests and forages on the ground.

COMMON YELLOWTHROAT
(Geothlypis trichas)

Description. Length 5 inches. Male olive-brown above, with yellow undersides and black facial mask. Female lacks black mask.
Distribution. Fairly common summer resident at all elevations among shrubby vegetation along streams and fencerows.
Remarks. Song is *witcity, wichity*.

HOODED WARBLER
(Wilsonia citrina)

Description. Length 5 inches. Male gray-green above, with yellow underparts, yellow face, black hood and throat. Female lacks black throat.
Distribution. Common summer resident in woodlands with undergrowth below 4,000 feet, particularly along brushy streams. Can often be found near Sugarlands and in the woodlands bordering Cades Cove.
Remarks. Does most of its foraging within 10 feet of the ground.

YELLOW-BREASTED CHAT
(Icteria virens)

Description. Length 7 inches. Dark brown above, with yellow undersides fading to white near tail. White eyebrow stripe. Thick bill.
Distribution. Fairly common summer resident up to 5,000 feet, but most abundant at lower elevations, primarily among thickets and brush.
Remarks. Sometimes sings at night.

Tanagers

These brightly colored birds are common in the tropics.

SUMMER TANAGER
(Piranga rubra)

Description. Length 8 inches. Male bright red. Female yellowish green.
Distribution. Fairly common summer resident below 2,000 feet. Prefers mature woodlands with pine, oak, and hickory.
Remarks. Forages high in the canopy, often hawking insects on the wing.

SCARLET TANAGER
(Piranga olivacea)

Description. Length 7 inches. Male all red except for black wings and tail. Female olive-yellow with black wings and tail.
Distribution. Common summer resident between 2,500 and 5,000 feet.
Remarks. Forages mostly in treetops.

Towhees and Sparrows

These are medium-size birds with conical bills. Eighteen species have been recorded in the park.

EASTERN TOWHEE
(Pipilo erythrophthalmus)

Description. Length 7 inches. Male has black upper parts, face, throat, and chest; rusty sides; white belly. Female has brownish upper parts, face, throat, and chest; rusty sides; white belly.
Distribution. Common resident up to 3,500 feet. Occasionally found at higher elevations among brushy openings in the forest.
Remarks. Forages on the ground. Formerly called the rufous-sided towhee.

CHIPPING SPARROW
(*Spizella passerina*)

Description. Length 5 inches. Back brown with streaks. Undersides whitish gray. Breeding adult has chestnut crown and eye stripe.
Distribution. Common summer resident below 3,000 feet where there are short grasses, such as lawns.
Remarks. Song is *chip, chip, chip*.

SONG SPARROW
(*Melospiza melodia*)

Description. Length 7 inches. Brown back, white undersides streaked with black on chest and sides; large, dark spot in center of breast. Long, rounded tail.
Distribution. Common resident of lower elevations with clearings and tangled underbrush near water. Occasionally seen at higher elevations in similar habitat. Can often be viewed near Elkmont, Oconaluftee, Sugarlands, and Cades Cove.
Remarks. Most variable North American sparrow, with thirty-one subspecies. Often a cowbird host.

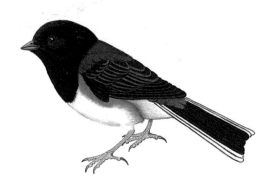

DARK-EYED JUNCO
(*Junco hyemalis*)

Description. Length 6 inches. Male generally gray with white belly. Female more brownish gray. Both have distinctive white outer-fringe tail feathers.
Distribution. Abundant resident below 3,000 feet in winter. Breeds at higher elevations in summer, becoming extremely common in the spruce-fir forest early in the season.
Remarks. The local population of juncos has a gray bill and is larger than other races.

Cardinals and Grosbeaks

These seedeaters have stout bills. Five species have been reported in the park, but only three breed there.

NORTHERN CARDINAL
(Cardinalis cardinalis)

Description. Length 9 inches. Male bright red with black face and chin. Female brown to olive. Both sexes have crest.
Distribution. Common resident below 3,500 feet in all kinds of habitat.
Remarks. Starts singing in January and continues through August. Even females sing.

ROSE-BREASTED GROSBEAK
(Pheucticus ludovicianus)

Description. Length 8 inches. Large, triangular bill. Male has rose red breast and white belly; black above with white wing and rump patches. Female brown overall, with streaked, buffy breast fading to whitish belly.
Distribution. Fairly common summer resident in northern hardwood forests between 3,500 and 5,000 feet, particularly among rhododendrons. Likely to be seen along Alum Cave and Chimney Tops Trails.
Remarks. Forages in mid to upper treetops.

Blackbirds

Despite the great variety in these birds, they all have pointed bills. Eight species have been reported in the park.

RED-WINGED BLACKBIRD
(Agelaius phoeniceus)

Description. Length 8 inches. Male black, with red and yellow shoulder patch. Female brown above, with heavily streaked underparts.
Distribution. Common summer resident in fields and along streams in Cades Cove.
Remarks. Males are territorial and defend their patches against intruders.

BROWN-HEADED COWBIRD
(Molothrus ater)

Description. Length 8 inches. Male has brown head and metallic green body. Female grayish brown above and lighter below.
Distribution. Fairly common resident below 2,000 feet.
Remarks. Nest parasite—lays eggs in the nests of other birds, which then raise the baby cowbirds as if they were their own.

Finches

Finches are seedeaters with an undulating flight. Eight species have been reported in the park, but only one is a common resident.

AMERICAN GOLDFINCH
(Carduelis tristis)

Description. Length 5 inches. Male yellow with black crown, wings, and tail. Female olive above; lacks black crown.
Distribution. Fairly common resident throughout the park, but more common below 4,500 feet. Watch for them along roadsides, where they feed on dandelion seeds.
Remarks. A late nester—doesn't even begin to build a nest until July or August, long after other birds have already fledged their young.

Mammals

Mammals evolved from an obscure group of reptiles known as Therapsida. They first appeared some 230 million years ago, about the time the great dinosaurs were beginning to populate the earth. The first mammals were tiny, no bigger than today's shrews. Then, with the extinction of the dinosaur some 65 million years ago, the mammal line suddenly exploded into many new and different forms. Modern mammals occupy every environment, from the great oceans of the world to the air in the tropics, and they vary in size from the blue whale to the tiniest shrew.

Despite this amazing diversity of life-forms, mammals share certain common traits. All mammals have hair, which not only insulates the body but also provides cryptic coloration and protects the skin. Mammals have mammary glands that secrete milk to nurture their young. Mammals also have highly developed and diversified teeth that perform many functions, from shearing to crushing. Finally, mammals possess a diaphragm for drawing air into the lungs. This additional air helps fuel the high body temperatures and activity rates of most mammals.

Most mammals in GSMNP are nocturnal and are not often seen, except by those who drive the back roads at night or walk the forest with a flashlight. Indeed, most of the smaller mammals are seen only if they happen to be found dead on the trail or road.

Species Accounts

In the descriptions that follow, length refers to the body and tail together. However, since the length of the tail is an important identifying characteristic for many species, tail length is also noted separately where appropriate.

Opossums

The opossum is the only marsupial in North America. All marsupials, including the kangaroo, koala bear, and other species common in Australia and South America, possess an external pouch where the young are carried and develop after birth.

VIRGINIA OPOSSUM
(Didelphis virginiana)

Description. Length up to 35 inches. Grayish white fur. Long, prehensile, sparsely haired tail. Sharp snout with pink nose.
Distribution. Found throughout the park, but most common at lower elevations.
Remarks. Opossums are omnivorous, feeding on everything from salamanders to millipedes. They have the shortest gestation period of any North American mammal—12.5 days. They will "play possum," or pretend to be dead, when threatened or frightened.

Shrews

Shrews are among the smallest mammals in North America. The pygmy shrew weighs only one-twelfth of an ounce. Shrews are ferocious predators and must consume large quantities of food. If deprived of food for even a day, they may starve to death. With their small bodies and active behavior, shrews burn up calories at a rapid rate—their hearts may beat up to 1,200 times a minute. Shrews have long, tapering snouts and tiny eyes and ears. Shrews rely on their highly developed senses of smell and touch to locate prey. Unlike the similar-looking moles, shrews' feet are all the same size. There are eight shrew species found in GSMNP.

MASKED SHREW
(Sorex cinerus)

Description. Length up to 4 inches. Tail up to 1.5 inches and slightly bicolored. Dark brown to gray-brown on back, with light gray underparts.

Distribution. Found among rotting logs, heavy leaf mold, and rocks in moist woods in a wide variety of elevations, up to the summit of Clingmans Dome. Other park locations where this shrew has been located include Greenbrier, Andrews Bald, Mount Guyot, Old Black Mountain, and Smokemont.

Remarks. Weaves 3- to 4-inch spherical nests of grass and other fibers that are hidden under logs and rocks.

SMOKY SHREW
(Sorex fumeus)

Description. Length up to 5 inches. Tail 1.5 to 2 inches, colored brown above and yellow below. Uniform brown color overall, including belly. In winter, the pelage changes to gray.

Distribution. Found at all elevations in cool, damp woods with a deep leaf layer on the ground, under logs, brush piles, and other cover, often near streams.

Remarks. The park is the southern limit of this species' natural range.

PYGMY SHREW
(Sorex hoyi)

Description. Length up to 3.5 inches. Tail approximately 1 inch and slightly bicolored. Fur grayish brown or reddish brown above and gray below. Smallest mammal in the world by weight.
Distribution. Found in deep leaf litter and under decaying logs in both deciduous and conifer forests.
Remarks. A northern species well distributed across the northern states from New England to Alaska. This species was only recently reported in the park along Foothills Parkway and at Newfound Gap.

NORTHERN WATER SHREW
(Sorex palustris)

Description. Length 6.5 inches. Tail 2.5 to 3 inches. Largest shrew in GSMNP. Blackish gray with white feet. Conspicuous fringe of stiff hairs on feet and toes.
Distribution. Always associated with water at mid elevations or higher. Lives along cold, swift mountain streams with overhanging vegetation. This northern species reaches its southern limit in GSMNP. Has been found along West Prong and Middle Prong of Little Pigeon River and Beech Flats Prong of Oconaluftee River.
Remarks. Swims and dives underwater to feed on aquatic insects, using its stiff hairs to propel itself through the water.

Moles

Moles are small rodents that live underground and are seldom observed on the surface. Their front feet, which are enlarged and look like paddles, are designed for digging and pushing aside dirt. Their soft fur can be brushed either forward or backward, facilitating movement in their subterranean tunnels. Their eyes are small, and their eyelids are fused together. There are three species of moles reported in GSMNP.

STAR-NOSED MOLE
(*Congylura cristata*)

Description. Length to 8.5 inches. Tail to 3.5 inches. Fur dark brown to black. Tail long and hairy. Most distinguishing feature is fingerlike protuberances that arise near the nose in a starlike pattern, giving rise to its common name.
Distribution. A northern species reaching its southern limit along the Appalachians, making it the least common mole in GSMNP. Prefers low, wet areas near streams, marshes, and swamps. Has been found as high as 5,300 feet along the Appalachian Trail, but most occurrences are lower.
Remarks. These moles are excellent swimmers and have even been observed swimming under ice in winter. Some of their burrows have underwater openings.

Bats

Bats resemble mice with wings, and they are the only mammals that can fly. Their forelimbs are adapted for flight with thin skin that stretches between what would otherwise be fingers. Bats' hearing is well developed, and echolocation is commonly used to find prey and for navigation. Bats often take insects on the wing, using their tails and wings to gather the insects, as well as capturing prey with their mouths. When insect populations decline in winter, bats must either hibernate or fly south to find food. There are ten species of bat recorded in GSMNP.

BIG BROWN BAT
(Eptesicus fuscus)

Description. Length to 5 inches. Wing-span 12 inches. Uniform dark brown fur above, paler below. Blackish ears are short and roundish.

Distribution. Found in a variety of habitats, including barns, churches, and other human habitation, as well as hollow trees and caves. Recorded in Cades Cove, Cosby, LeConte Lodge, Cataloochee, and park headquarters.

Remarks. Largest bat in GSMNP. These bats are colonial, often hibernating in aggregations of 100 or more.

SILVER-HAIRED BAT
(Lasionycteris noctivagans)

Description. Length to 4 inches. Tail 1 to 1.75 inches. Fur dark brown; hairs on back often tipped with silver. Ears short and pushed forward, barely reaching tip of nose.

Distribution. Typically seen only during migration in spring and fall. Usually found at lower elevations. Has been reported in Cades Cove, park head-quarters, Meigs Creek, and Greenbrier.

Remarks. This northern bat is not known to breed in the park. Flight tends to be slow and fluttery, with numerous rapid changes in direction.

HOARY BAT
(*Lasiurus cinereus*)

Description. Length to 6 inches. Tail 2 to 2.5 inches. Fur yellow-brown to mahogany brown, but tipped with white, resembling silver frosting. Rims of ears dark brown.

Distribution. Strongly migratory, though some may be year-round residents. Typically found in forested areas, often roosting in trees.

Remarks. One of the last bats to appear in the evening, typically leaving its roost only after sunset. Moths are its primary prey.

SMALL-FOOTED MYOTIS
(*Myotis leibii*)

Description. Length to 3 inches. Tail 1 to 1.5 inches. Fur light brown. Black ears and face mask.

Distribution. Typically found in caves or among rocks in forests. Only a few of these bats have been recorded in the park, at park headquarters and at Greenbrier Cove.

Remarks. Smallest member of the genus *Myotis* in North America. Rarest bat in the GSMNP and one of the rarest in the eastern United States.

LITTLE BROWN BAT
(Myotis lucifugus)

Description. Length to 4 inches. Tail 1 to 1.75 inches. Fur brownish with glossy sheen. Wings, tail, and ears dark brown. Ears reach nose when laid forward.
Distribution. Found beneath bark on trees, in hollow trees, in crevices, and in buildings. In GSMNP, this bat has been reported at Elkmont, Hazel Creek Ranger Station, Cataloochee, Myhr Cave, and Bull Cave.
Remarks. Colonial, with maternity sites sometimes harboring several thousand bats. Longest life span of any bat, with some individuals living thirty years or more.

Rabbits

Rabbits are members of the order Lagomorpha, which includes rabbits, hares, and pikas. Rabbits have long ears, large feet, and small, short tails. They hop from place to place. They spend most of the day hidden in brush piles and among other dense vegetation, venturing forth at night to forage. They are primarily vegetarian, feeding on bark, grass, and flowers. Only two species of rabbit are found in GSMNP.

APPALACHIAN COTTONTAIL
(Sylvilagus obscurus)

Description. Length to 18 inches. Fur reddish brown to grayish brown with black highlights on back. Underparts grayish white.
Distribution. Prefers thick, dense woods. Few reports from the park, partly because it closely resembles the more common eastern cottontail. Has been observed by Elkmont and the Alum Cave parking area.
Remarks. This rabbit was formerly known as the New England cottontail.

Chipmunks, Woodchucks, and Squirrels

These animals are all rodents with specialized teeth for gnawing.

EASTERN CHIPMUNK
(*Tamias striatus*)

Description. Length to 10 inches. Tail 3 to 4 inches. Fur reddish brown, with five blackish dorsal stripes fringing two white stripes along upper sides and back. White facial stripes on either side of eye. Underparts white. Internal cheek pouches for storing food.

Distribution. Found near edge habitat in hardwood forests, including the fringes of balds, cliffs, and farmlands. Reported throughout the park, all the way up into the spruce-fir forests on Clingmans Dome and Mount Guyot, but less numerous in this habitat.

Remarks. Hibernates during colder months. Diet is chiefly seeds, acorns, and fruit. Carries food in cheek pouches for later caching in underground storage chambers.

WOODCHUCK
(*Marmota monax*)

Description. Length to 27 inches. Tail 4 to 7 inches. Fur brown, sometimes with grizzled appearance. Heavy body with short limbs. Broad, flattened head; blunt nose; short, rounded ears.

Distribution. Prefers open meadows and is most abundant at lower elevations along roadsides and among the fields in Cades Cove.

Remarks. Hibernates four to five months of the year. Emits a loud whistle when alarmed.

GRAY SQUIRREL
(Sciurus carolinensis)

Description. Length to 22 inches. Tail 6 to 10 inches. Fur mostly gray above, with silver gray below. Tinges of brown on head, sides, and back. Bushy tail.
Distribution. Prefers hardwood forests, especially trees with mast, such as beeches and oaks.
Remarks. Constructs nests of leaves and grass in tree cavities and forks of trees.

NORTHERN FLYING SQUIRREL
(Glaucomys sabrinus)

Description. Length to 11 inches. Tail to 5 inches. Fur brown above, white underneath. Large eyes. Broad, flattened tail.
Distribution. Reaches its southern limit in the Appalachians. Prefers spruce-fir and northern hardwood forests of higher elevations.
Remarks. Recently classified as endangered in the southern Appalachians. Nests in hollow tree cavities and old woodpecker holes.

Beavers

The beaver is the largest rodent in North America and can weigh more than sixty pounds. Beavers are semiaquatic, readily swimming underwater. They have webbed feet and ears and noses that shut when the animal is immersed. The flat, scaly tail is a distinctive feature. Beavers are well known for their habit of building dams on streams to create ponds.

AMERICAN BEAVER
(*Castor canadensis*)

Description. Length to 60 inches. Tail 12 inches. Dark brown fur. Small ears.
Distribution. Found along streams. Observed in Cades Cove, Fontana Lake, and other lower-elevation areas of the park.
Remarks. By the turn of the twentieth century, beavers had been extirpated from the region by trapping pressure. They have gradually recovered and can be found in a number of park locations.

Rats and Mice

Rats and mice constitute one of the largest groups of mammals represented in GSMNP. Given the variety, it is difficult to generalize about their characteristics, but most members are terrestrial and nocturnal.

DEER MOUSE
(*Peromyscus maniculatus*)

Description. Length to 9 inches. Tail to 4.25 inches. Reddish brown to brownish gray above, with white belly and feet. Tail bicolored, with white below and dark brown above. Large eyes and ears.
Distribution. Prefers grassy areas and cool, moist forests. Most abundant at higher elevations, typically above 3,000 feet.
Remarks. Staple prey for many predators, from owls to weasels.

ALLEGHENY WOOD RAT
(*Neotoma magister*)

Description. Length to 17 inches. Tail to 8 inches. Brownish gray above, with white throat, belly, and feet. Large ears and eyes.

Distribution. Prefers caves and rocky cliffs, as well as abandoned buildings. Recorded in Cataloochee, Tremont, and Abrams Creek and near Fontana Reservoir.

Remarks. Wood rats pile up heaps of sticks and debris to create large mounds that may be 10 feet across and 4 to 5 feet high.

Voles and Muskrats

RED-BACKED VOLE
(*Clethrionomys gapperi*)

Description. Length to 6.5 inches. Tail to 2 inches. Reddish back, gray sides, silver belly. Short tail. Small eyes.

Distribution. Prefers moist woodlands. Found under mossy logs and boulders. Recorded at Bote Mountain, Buck Prong, Eagle Rock Creek, Low Gap, Walker Prong, Newfound Gap, Clingmans Dome, and Mount Guyot.

Remarks. This northern species, found across Canada, reaches its southern limit in the Appalachians in the vicinity of GSMNP.

COMMON MUSKRAT
(Ondatra zibethica)

Description. Length to 25 inches. Tail to 11 inches. Upper body covered with soft brown fur. Underparts white or light brown. Eyes and ears small. Hind feet partially webbed. Laterally compressed tail for swimming.

Distribution. Common in GSMNP below 2,500 feet. Semiaquatic, so strongly associated with streams, marshes, and other bodies of water. Recorded at Greenbrier, Cosby, Cades Cove, Elkmont, and Oconaluftee River.

Remarks. Not a rat at all, but a large vole. Males emit a musky secretion from glands, giving rise to the popular name.

Canids

Canids include the doglike species such as foxes, coyotes, and wolves. They all have large, erect ears and long, bushy tails. Four species of canids are occasionally found in GSMNP—the gray fox, red fox, coyote, and red wolf. Wolves were native to the park area but were extirpated by the late 1800s. Attempts to reestablish wolf populations began in the 1990s, with the introduction of the endangered red wolf in 1991. The experiment was terminated due to conflicts with livestock and surrounding landowners, along with low survival rates of young. Whether there will be further attempts at restoration is not known.

COYOTE
(Canis latrans)

Description. Length to 53 inches. Tail to 15 inches. Color varies from gray to rusty red, with white throat and belly. Bushy tail.

Distribution. Found throughout the park in low numbers.

Remarks. Coyotes only recently colonized the park, with the first specimen positively identified in 1982.

RED FOX
(Vulpes vulpes)

Description. Length to 42 inches. Tail 16 inches. Doglike. Fur reddish orange, with black feet and legs. Underparts whitish. Very bushy tail with white tip. Muzzle narrow and delicate. Ears pointed and erect.

Distribution. Typically associated with edges along farmland intermixed with woods, but its presence has been recorded throughout GSMNP, including at Cosby, Becks Bald, Indian Gap, Mount LeConte, and Greenbrier Cove.

Remarks. The red fox is monogamous and may remain mated for life.

GRAY FOX
(Urocyon cinereoargenteus)

Description. Length to 44 inches. Tail to 17 inches. Doglike. Fur gray with black highlights, fading to light reddish gray on sides. Patches of white on throat, chest, and belly. Bushy tail has black tip.

Distribution. Common in woodlands at lower elevations, although occasionally found higher. Recorded in Cades Cove, Smokemont, Elkmont, and Big Creek.

Remarks. This fox climbs trees and easily leaps from branch to branch.

Black bears are found throughout GSMNP. The park is a major refuge for the bear in the Southeast, where poaching outside of the park has depressed some populations.

Bears

Bears are omnivorous and eat a wide variety of foods, although the majority of their diet is vegetarian. They have small eyes and ears and very short tails. The only bear found in GSMNP is the black bear. In other parts of the country, black bears come in a variety of colors, including cinnamon, blonde, red, and even white, but in GSMNP, all black bears are black. Although bears may be active throughout the year, most of them den and hibernate for part of the winter. Bears are not true hibernators, however, because they can be awakened and roused easily. Many bears select large hollow trees for denning, demonstrating the ecological value of old-growth forest stands with abundant snags for black bear survival.

BLACK BEAR
(*Ursus americanus*)

Description. Length to 72 inches. Tail to 5 inches. Fur typically glossy black. Brown muzzle. Many bears have a white patch on chest.
Distribution. Found throughout GSMNP.
Remarks. The average black bear seldom weighs more than 200 to 250 pounds, with males considerably larger than females. Individuals 700 pounds or more have been reported in North America.

Raccoons

Racoons are easily recognized by their black facial masks and handlike paws. They are omnivorous and eat a variety of foods, including berries, crayfish, frogs, small birds, and eggs.

RACCOON
(*Procyon lotor*)

Description. Length to 41 inches. Tail to 12 inches. Fur a mixture of brown, black, and gray, creating an overall brownish gray coloration. Black face mask across eyes. Tail bushy with black rings.
Distribution. Found throughout the park, but strongly associated with streams and rivers.
Remarks. Readily climbs trees. Den is typically found in hollow trees.

Baby raccoons.

Mustelids

Members of the weasel family include the fisher, mink, weasel, skunk, and otter. Most mustelids have long bodies, short legs, and scent glands (with those of the skunk best known). Five members of this family have been recorded in GSMNP. The status of a sixth, the fisher, is uncertain. It may have occurred within the boundaries of the park at one time, but no records exist.

LONG-TAILED WEASEL
(Mustela frenata)

Description. Length to 17 inches. Tail to 6 inches. Long, thin body. Dark glossy brown above, with yellow-white breast and belly. Black-tipped tail.
Distribution. Found in a wide variety of habitats at all elevations. Has been recorded at Sugarlands, Greenbrier Cove, Mount LeConte, Cataloochee, and Little River.
Remarks. Very active and alert, often curious.

MINK
(Mustela vison)

Description. Length to 26 inches. Tail to 9 inches. Fur dark chocolate brown, with white patches on chin and throat. Tail well furred; seldom more than half of body length.
Distribution. Rare in GSMNP, but found at all elevations. Prefers brush and forested areas along rivers, streams, and swamps.
Remarks. Minks are excellent swimmers, spending much of their time in the water chasing fish, crayfish, and frogs.

RIVER OTTER
(Lutra canadensis)

Description. Length to 50 inches. Tail 19 inches. Fur dark brown overall. Slender body; short legs. Head broad and flat. Ears small. Feet webbed.

Distribution. Found along streams and rivers.

Remarks. The otter was extirpated from GSMNP, but a reintroduction program begun in the 1980s has reestablished this playful, active animal in park waters.

The river otter was recently reintroduced into GSMNP.

STRIPED SKUNK
(Mephitis mephitis)

Description. Length to 30 inches. Tail 12 inches. Cat size. Bold black and white striping from head down back. Bushy black and white tail.
Distribution. Agricultural areas with brushy or wooded patches are ideal habitat. Has been recorded at Smokemont, Cades Cove, Newfound Gap, Greenbrier Cove, and Elkmont.
Remarks. Larger of the two skunks found in GSMNP.

SPOTTED SKUNK
(Spilogale putorius)

Description. Length to 23 inches. Tail 8 inches. Black with white spots on forehead and under ears. Broken white stripes on back, sides, and neck. White-tipped tail.
Distribution. Found at lower elevations than the striped skunk. Prefers agricultural areas with patches of woodlands. Common around cliffs and rock slides.
Remarks. Smaller of the two skunks found in GSMNP.

Cats

All cats have short faces and small ears and are active year-round. They stalk their prey, as opposed to running it down like wolves. Of the native cats, only bobcats are definitively found in GSMNP. Mountain lions were once native to the area but were extirpated.

*Bobcat kitten
in tree cavity.*

BOBCAT
(Lynx rufus)

Description. Length to 40 inches. Tail to 6 inches. Short, broad face with ruff of fur along cheeks and jaw. Pointed ears with tufts. Back of ear has white spot bordered by black. Fur generally light brown, with mixture of black and brown hairs. Black-tipped tail.

Distribution. Prefers woodlands at all elevations in GSMNP. Has been recorded at Twentymile Creek, Smokemont, Cades Cove, Greenbrier Cove, Mount LeConte, and Clingmans Dome.

Remarks. Bobcats mark their territories, leaving scent posts that include feces.

Deer and Elk

Both deer and elk are hoofed animals with antlers that are shed annually (as opposed to horns, which are not).

WHITE-TAILED DEER
(*Odocoileus virginianus*)

Description. Length to 71 inches. Tail to 12 inches. Fur light gray-brown to reddish brown, depending on season. Throat and underparts white. White tail. Curving antlers on males.

Distribution. Found throughout the park, but most common in Cades Cove and other open areas.

Remarks. When alarmed, deer flash and wag their white tails to signal other members of the herd and to disorient any trailing predator.

White-tailed deer fawn. The best place to see white-tailed deer is open meadow lands such as those found in Cades Cove.

ELK
(Cervus elaphus)

Description. Length to 120 inches. Height at shoulder 5 feet. Dark fur on neck and head, with light tan sides and back. Males have antlers up to 4 feet long, with up to seven prongs each.

Distribution. Prefers openings and forested glades.

Remarks. Elks were native to the park but were extirpated by 1750. They were recently reintroduced, but their numbers are still low. The first calf born in the park in 150 years was discovered in June 2001.

Hiking Guide

One of the best ways to get to know GSMNP is to take a walk. With more than 900 miles of trails, there are opportunities for everything from a short stroll in the woods to a multiday backpack trek. Most of the trails were once roads, old railroad grades, and pioneer routes. There are more than 100 backcountry campsites available, but if you do plan to camp overnight, discuss your plans with park managers to ensure that you have the latest information, including permits and regulations. You should also practice minimum-impact camping techniques. If you don't know what these are, ask the Park Service for guidance.

Although characterized by a mild climate, keep in mind that the Smokies are very wet, and hypothermia is a real danger. In addition, remember that higher elevations can be considerably cooler than low-elevation trailheads. Be prepared for inclement weather, and take the appropriate gear.

One of the thrills of hiking in GSMNP is the opportunity to see wildlife in its natural surroundings. The most popular yet feared animal is the black bear. Most black bears are docile and will not attack humans, but the important qualifier is "most." If you want to avoid problems, the paramount rule is to keep food away from bears. With few exceptions, nearly all lethal bear attacks have been by animals that had grown accustomed to human food. Proper storage of food is therefore essential. In campgrounds, keep all food not in immediate use inside vehicles or in other bear-proof containers. When camping in the backcountry, hang all food and other scented items such as toothpaste in a tree at least 15 feet off the ground. The Park Service can provide advice on how to hang food.

If you happen to encounter a bear on the trail, you probably have nothing to fear. Enjoy the view if you're not too close to the animal. Bears are interesting and intelligent creatures, and watching them can be a

Hikers on Andrews Bald view the summer-time haze resulting from the transpiration of water vapor from the lush vegetation. This haze gives the mountains its name—the Smokies. More recently human-caused smog from power plants has added to the mix, causing acid rainfall that not only obscures scenic vistas, but also threatens park plants and animals.

memorable experience. Most bears would just as soon leave you alone and will generally run away at the first scent or sight of a person. If, for some reason, this doesn't happen, watch the bear for signs of distress. Chomping and grinding of teeth, erect ears, huffing, and growling are all indications that the bear is not pleased by your presence. In this situation, it's best to leave, but *don't run*. Bears, as predators, are conditioned to chase prey. By running, you signal that you are prey—and this is not the message you want to communicate. If the bear is watching you or approaching you, back away slowly, talking quietly to the bear to reassure it of your nonhostile intentions.

Even if the bear races toward you, it doesn't necessarily mean that an attack is imminent. Bears have notoriously poor eyesight. It may be coming closer for a better look or, in some cases, to bluff-charge you. Often, the best thing you can do is simply stand your ground.

If you are attacked, drop to the ground on your stomach, put your hands behind your head to protect your neck, and try to remain calm—obviously not an easy thing to do. But remember that most bears are merely trying to frighten you, not eat you.

The only other serious threats are snakes. There are two poisonous snakes in GSMNP—the rattlesnake and the copperhead. Most snakebites are nonlethal. If you are bitten and you have a companion, remain calm and send him or her for help. If you must walk, do so slowly, with frequent stops.

Most of the trails in the park are well marked, and a map isn't a necessity, but it doesn't hurt to have a good map and a compass if you'll be venturing far from the roads, especially if you are planning a long hike. If you should get lost, keep in mind that traveling downhill almost anyplace in the park will eventually lead you to a road. It may not be the quickest or easiest route, but sooner or later, you will reach a road or at least a reservoir with boats. In any event, help won't be far off.

Following is a brief sampling of some of the trails in the park. This list is by no means exhaustive. For more detailed descriptions of the hikes, a number of good hiking guides are available.

Appalachian Trail

The best-known trail is the 2,143-mile Appalachian Trail from Georgia to Maine, with 68.6 miles traversing the park. GSMNP boasts the highest point on the trail (Clingmans Dome) and the longest stretch above 5,000 feet (34 miles). The trail offers access to some of the best features of the park, including examples of its major plant communities, geology, and wildlife, plus views at outcrops and balds. There are trail shelters every 7 to 8 miles, all with chain-link fences to keep bears out. Stays in these shelters are restricted to one night and must be reserved in advance. Although numerous other trails intersect the Appalachian Trail, the best place to do a day hike or even start a backpack trek is probably Newfound Gap on the cross-park road.

Trails from Cades Cove

Anthony Creek Trail: This 3.5-mile trail starts near the Cades Cove picnic area and climbs to Bote Mountain Trail. It follows Anthony Creek, a dashing stream. There are some large hemlocks along the lower portion of the trail, and the higher sections offer good views of Cades Cove in winter. This trail also provides access to Russell Field Trail. Russell Field is a bald at the crest of the Smokies along the Appalachian Trail with outstanding views.

Rich Mountain Loop Trail: The trailhead is just beyond the entrance to the Cades Cove Loop Road. The 7.4-mile trail climbs to the top of Rich Mountain via Crooked Arm Ridge, then follows the crest of the mountain. Along this stretch there are blooming wildflowers in spring, as well as scenic views. It descends via Indian Grave Gap Trail and Rich Mountain Loop Trail past John Oliver's historic cabin.

Abrams Falls Trail: The trailhead is located at the far end of the Cades Cove Loop. The 4.2-mile trail follows Abrams Creek to Abrams Falls, which drops 20 feet over a lip of sandstone. The trail also connects to other trails in this end of Cades Cove, making it one of the most popular trails in the park.

Rabbit Creek Trail: This 7.6-mile trail starts at the same place as Abrams Falls Trail and ends at Abrams Creek Campground. It is more or less level, but crossing the stream is required, so be prepared.

Gregory Bald via Gregory Ridge: Some consider this one of the finest hikes in GSMNP. It's 4.9 miles from the end of Forge Creek Road to Gregory Bald. Forge Creek Road is just past Cable Mill turnoff on Cades Cove Loop Road. The trail passes an old-growth forest along Forge Creek. It then goes steeply up a ridge and keeps ascending to Gregory Bald, a high meadow with a 360-degree view. In June, the world's finest display of flame azalea colors the clearing, and there is spectacular color in autumn.

Trails on Parson Branch Road

Gregory Bald Trail: It's 4.5 miles to Gregory Bald. The trailhead is located at Sam's Gap, along the Parson Branch Road. The trailhead lies at 2,780 feet, and Gregory Bald is at 4,950 feet. Gregory Bald has spectacular azalea displays in June. It's possible to continue another 3.1 miles beyond the bald to the Appalachian Trail at Doe Knob.

Hannah Mountain Trail: It's 7.6 miles from Sam's Gap to Rabbit Creek Trail. The trailhead is at Sam's Gap and follows ridges through dry forests of oak and hickory, until descending to Rabbit Creek.

Trails Near Twentymile Ranger Station

Twentymile Trail: It's 4.7 miles from the ranger station to the Appalachian Trail at Sassafras Gap. The Twentymile Ranger Station is one of the most remote in the park. The trail is an old railroad grade constructed by the Kitchens Lumber Company. Part of the trail follows Proctor Branch, a beautiful cascading trout stream.

Wolf Ridge Trail: It's 6.4 miles to Gregory Bald Trail. Wolf Ridge Trail is an old railroad grade constructed by timber companies to get logs from the mountains to the mills. The trail passes through Parsons Bald, which features blooming azaleas in June.

Twentymile Loop: This loop is 15.6 miles. Start at Twentymile Ranger Station and hike up Twentymile Trail to Twentymile Cascades. Continue on Twentymile Creek to the Upper Flats streamside camp among cove hardwoods. On day two, climb onto Long Hungry Ridge and take this to Gregory Bald. Enjoy the majesty of the southern Appalachians, including terrific views and a rich floral display in late June. Camp at nearby Sheep Pen Gap, a grassy, high-country flat shaded by yellow birch that lies between Gregory Bald and Parson Bald. Leave the grassy balds and complete the loop via the steep Wolf Ridge Trail.

Trails Near Fontana Reservoir

Lakeshore Trail: This trail accesses some of the more remote sections of the park along Fontana Reservoir. It begins at Fontana Dam and ends at Lakeshore Drive or the Road to Nowhere. It is often hiked in sections, but the total length of the trail is nearly 42 miles, offering a great multi-day hike if a shuttle can be arranged. Among the larger drainages crossed by the trail are Forney Creek, Hazel Creek, and Eagle Creek. Highlights include views of Fontana Lake, historic sites, good fishing, and solitude in some sections.

Trails Near Deep Creek

Indian Creek Trail: It's 3.9 miles from Deep Creek Trail to Martin Gap Trail. You must hike 0.7 mile on Deep Creek Trail to access this trail. It is an old road that follows the creek for most of its distance, passing Indian Creek Falls, a 60-foot drop into a lovely pool. The sites of old homesteads are slowly being taken back by forest.

Deep Creek Trail: It's 14.7 miles from Deep Creek Road to Newfound Gap Road. This trail was constructed largely through virgin forest. It is well graded and maintained. Lovely hemlock forests, along with large hardwoods such as yellow poplar and yellow birch, are common. If you have a choice, it's best to start at Newfound Gap and walk downhill to Deep Creek Road.

Sunkota Ridge Trail: It's 8.6 miles to Thomas Divide Trail. Access the trail from Deep Creek Loop Trail. Good views are available, particularly in winter.

Trails Near Smokemont

Smokemont Loop: The Bradley Fork–Smokemont Loop is 5.7 miles. The trailhead is located in the Smokemont Campground. This easy trail passes through nice forests and climbs Richland Mountain, with old cemeteries and old home sites along the way.

Hughes Ridge Trail: This 11.8-mile trail begins by the Smokemont Church and follows Hughes Ridge to the Appalachian Trail. Most of the elevation gain is in the first few miles. There are good views on this path, but little water.

Newton Bald Trail: This 4.8-mile trail starts opposite the Smokemont Campground and climbs 2,000 feet to Newton Bald. There are good views on top of the ridge.

Trails Near Raven Fork

Hyatt Bald Trail: It's 2.9 miles to the bald, and 4.5 miles to the McGee Spring campsite. The trail starts on Straight Fork Road and ends at Hyatt Bald, at 5,153 feet. The bald was once grazed by cattle but is now wooded. It's a steep climb. This hike can be turned into a loop by continuing down Beech Gap Trail.

Beech Gap Trail 1: This 2.5-mile trail starts at Round Bottom on Straight Fork Road and climbs to Beech Gap on Balsam Mountain Trail.

Beech Gap Trail 11: This 2.9-mile trail also begins at Round Bottom on Straight Fork Road. It climbs to Hyatt Ridge Trail and is the other half of the loop with Hyatt Bald Trail.

Balsam Ridge Trail: It's 10.1 miles from Balsam Mountain Road to the Appalachian Trail at Tricorner Knob. This is a high-elevation trail that passes through spruce-fir forest on a connecting ridge between the Smokies and the Balsams. The trailhead is on Balsam Mountain Road at Pin Oak Gap.

Trails Near Cataloochee

Palmer Creek Trail: It's 4.6 miles from the trailhead on Cataloochee Road and Pin Oak Gap on Balsam Mountain Road. The trail, once an old road, follows the creek most of the way. The upper sections offer views of the Cataloochee Valley.

Little Cataloochee Trail: The trail is 5.2 miles. It was once an old road that connected Little Cataloochee and Cataloochee Valleys, passing over Cooks Knob.

Rough Fork Trail: This 6.5-mile trail begins on Cataloochee Road and climbs to Polls Gap at 5,130 feet.

Caldwell Fork Trail: This 6.5-mile trail starts near the Cataloochee Campground and follows Caldwell Fork for most of the climb up to Rough Fork Trail. Some large trees left from logging days can be seen along this path.

Cataloochee Divide Trail: This 11.5-mile trail is mostly a ridge hike. It begins on Cove Creek Road and follows the park's southeastern boundary. It ends at Polls Gap on Balsam Mountain Road. The highest point is 5,540 feet at Hemphill Bald. There are good views on this path.

Trails Near Big Creek

Big Creek Trail: This 5.9-mile trail begins at Big Creek Campground and ends at Camel Gap Trail by Walnut Bottoms. It follows the creek all the way, providing beautiful views through a rich bottomland forest.

Big Creek Loop: The loop totals 16.9 miles of good views, old-growth forest, and some fine fishing. Start at Big Creek Ranger Station and follow an old road on a gentle grade 5.3 miles to Walnut Bottoms campsite. Several streams join here, providing fishing opportunities. Then climb

Swallow Fork Trail 4 miles to Mount Sterling Ridge. Once on the ridge, enjoy 1.4 miles of fine hiking through spruce-fir forest to Mount Sterling and the highest unsheltered backcountry campsite in the park, at 5,800 feet. Descend 6.2 miles through some fine old-growth forest along the very steep Baxter Creek Trail back to Big Creek.

Hiker on the Cataloochee Divide Trail.

Baxter Creek Trail: This is a steep, rocky, 6.2-mile trail that begins in Big Creek Campground and ends at the top of Mount Sterling. The final mile or so passes through moss-covered spruce-fir forest and a high-elevation campsite at 5,800 feet.

Chestnut Branch Trail: This 2-mile trail begins by the Big Creek Ranger Station and connects to the Appalachian Trail, with access to Mount Cammerer some 3.9 miles beyond.

Trails Near Cosby

Lower Mount Cammerer Trail: It's 7.4 miles from Cosby Campground to the Appalachian Trail. This trail offers views from Sutton Ridge and can be used to access the Appalachian Trail and then Mount Cammerer, 2.3 miles beyond. This trail dips in and out of streams on the side of Mount Cammerer.

Maddron Bald Loop: The loop totals 17.2 miles. Some consider this one of the best overnight trips in the park. Start along the lower reaches of Gabes Mountain, passing Henwallow Falls, and enter virgin woodland to camp at Sugar Cove. Head up Maddron Bald Trail to Albright Grove, which contains some of the largest old-growth trees in the park. Camp along Otter Creek near Maddron Bald, and enjoy the view. Return via Snake Den Trail.

Gabes Mountain Trail: This 7-mile trail begins by the Cosby Campground. It passes Henwallow Falls and ends at Maddron Bald Trail. Giant trees are encountered along the way.

Low Gap Trail: This short (2.9-mile) but steep trail connects Cosby Creek Road by the Cosby Campground with Low Gap on the Appalachian Trail. It passes through a nice forest of eastern hemlock with some large trees.

Trails Near Greenbrier

Ramsay Cascade Trail: The trailhead is located along Greenbrier Road. This 4-mile trail passes through beautiful forest, with some large trees left behind from logging days. The trail ends at Ramsay Cascade, a high waterfall.

Old Settler's Trail: This 15.9-mile trail starts on Ramsay Cascade Road and ends at Maddron Bald Trail. It connects the Greenbrier area to the Cosby area trail system, passing many historic sites along the way and crossing more than a dozen small creeks.

• **Porter's Gap Trail:** The trailhead is at the junction of Greenbrier and Ramsey Fork Roads. The 3.7-mile trail ends at a backcountry campsite. The area is well known for its wildflower displays in April and May. The creek is scenic, tumbling over large, mossy boulders. Fern Falls, 40 feet high, is reached at 1.9 miles.

Brushy Mountain Trail: This 5.6-mile trail climbs to Brushy Mountain, a heath bald near Trillium Gap on Mount LeConte. The trailhead begins where the Greenbrier and Ramsey Fork Roads meet and follows Porter Creek Trail for the first mile before veering off.

Trails Near Roaring Fork and LeConte

Baskins Creek Trail: This 2.7-mile trail connects Roaring Fork Road with Trillium Gap Trail by Cherokee Orchard Road. The 25-foot Baskins Falls is seen along the way. This seldom-hiked trail offers solitude.

Grapeyard Ridge Trail: This 7.6-mile trail connects Roaring Fork Road to Greenbrier Road, with one backcountry campsite along the way. Hemlock forest and lots of rhododendrons make this a pleasant hike, particularly in June.

• **Rainbow Falls Trail:** The trailhead is on Cherokee Orchard Road. This 6.6-mile trail climbs past Rainbow Falls and then steeply to the summit of Mount LeConte. You reach Rainbow Falls at about 2.4 miles. The falls cascade 80 feet over a series of ledges in a fine spray.

Trails from Newfound Gap Road

• **Old Sugarlands Trail:** This lightly used trail is 3.9 miles long. It begins by the Sugarlands visitor center parking area and travels along the Middle Prong of the Little Pigeon River. It ends near the Bullhead trailhead by Cherokee Orchard Road.

• **Husky Gap Trail:** This 4.1-mile trail begins along Newfound Gap Road, 1.7 miles south of the Sugarlands visitor center. It climbs 2 miles to Husky Gap and then descends 2.1 miles to the Little River near Elkmont.

Cove Mountain Trail: This 8.6-mile trail begins by park headquarters and climbs along the park boundary to Cove Mountain fire tower. You can make it a one-way hike with a shuttle by continuing from Cove Mountain by way of Laurel Falls Trail to Little River Road.

Chimney Tops Trail: The trailhead is 7.5 miles south of Sugarlands on Newfound Gap Road. The 2-mile trail first climbs down to cross the West

Grotto Falls in the Roaring Fork drainage.

Prong of the Little River, then climbs to the Chimney Tops—bare rocks offering good views. This is one of the most popular trails in the park.

Alum Cave Bluffs Trail: This 5-mile trail begins 9 miles from Sugarlands on Newfound Gap Road and leads to Mount LeConte. It is the shortest route to the top of LeConte, and many believe that it has the finest scenery of any trail in the park.

Trails Near Elkmont

Jakes Creek Trail: It's 3.3 miles to Jakes Gap. The trail follows noisy Jakes Creek via an old railroad grade. The creamy white blossoms of Fraser magnolia make this hike a treat in the spring.

❧ **Meigs Creek Trail:** It's 3.5 miles from Sinks to Meigs Mountain Trail. The trail crosses Meigs Creek numerous times and passes many small cascades, as well as a lovely 20-foot waterfall that tumbles over mossy rocks to a plunge pool. The trail ends at Buckhorn Gap, with its old-growth hemlock trees.

Rapids along the West Prong of Little Pigeon River.

• **Laurel Falls Trail:** This 4-mile trail is one of the most popular in the park, offering easy access to the 75-foot cascade of Laurel Falls. It is 1.3 miles to the falls; the trail then continues on to connect with Cove Mountain Trail. The trailhead is found at Fighting Gap on Little River Road.

Little River Loop: The loop totals 13.4 miles The trailhead lies just upstream from the Elkmont Campground. This trip offers creekside and ridgeline camping, with a fair amount of climbing in between. First follow

Laurel Falls is a popular destination.

the splashing waters of Little River through lovely forests for 3 miles to Rough Creek camp. From this campsite, climb Rough Creek Trail 2.8 miles on an old railroad grade to Sugarland Mountain Trail. Follow this approximately 4 miles to the next stop at Medicine Branch Bluff campsite. From there, take Husky Gap Trail 2.1 miles back to Little River and your starting point.

Trails Near Clingmans Dome Road

Forney Ridge Trail: This 5.7-mile trail starts by the Clingmans Dome parking lot and descends Forney Ridge to its junction with Springhouse Branch Trail. The most popular section of the trail is the 1.8 miles to Andrews Bald, which provides terrific views of the North Carolina mountains. The bald features flame azalea and Catawba rhododendron blooms in late June.

Forney Creek Trail: This 10.3-mile trail starts at the Clingmans Dome parking area and descends all the way to Lakeshore Trail on Fontana Lake. The first 1.1 miles follows Forney Ridge Trail before veering off to drop into the Forney Creek drainage, which it follows the rest of the way to the lake. There are a number of backcountry campsites. Or, if a shuttle has been arranged, you could hike Lakeshore Trail to Lakeshore Drive to complete a long day hike.

Fork Ridge Trail: The trailhead lies at 5,880 feet, about 3.7 miles up Clingmans Dome Road. The 5.1-mile trail begins in spruce forest, descends to Poke Patch on Deep Creek Trail, and ends in hardwood forest.

Silers Bald via Appalachian Trail: It's 4.8 miles to the Silers Bald shelter from the Clingmans Dome parking lot. This trail starts high and stays high, undulating along the crest of the Smokies. There are great views at Silers Bald.

Clingmans Dome Road Loop: The loop totals 36 miles. This trip requires spending several nights at backcountry camps and exposes you to all the park's ecosystems. You'll find good fishing in Hazel Creek and great views on the Appalachian Trail, plus you'll encounter some of the wilder parts of the park. Start at Clingmans Dome and head to Silers Bald (as above), then take Welch Ridge Trail to Hazel Creek Trail. Go down Hazel Creek Trail to Cold Springs Gap Trail. Take Cold Springs Gap Trail to Bear Creek Trail and over to Forney Creek. Follow Forney Creek up to Clingmans Dome Road and your starting point.

Nearby Areas

Cherokee Indian Reservation

The 56,000-acre Cherokee Indian Reservation is immediately adjacent to GSMNP in North Carolina. It is home to the eastern band of Cherokee, who evaded capture and deportation to Oklahoma in the 1830s. Those traveling Newfound Gap Road or Highway 441 pass through the reservation. There are numerous accommodations and places to eat in Cherokee, and the tribe operates a visitor center there. One of the attractions within the reservation is the Museum of the Cherokee Indian, with exhibits of Cherokee artifacts as well as history. To see how the Cherokee Indians lived, visit the Oconaluftee Indian Village and witness demonstrations of traditional skills, including weaving, basket making, and pottery. *Unto These Hills* is a theatrical performance that traces Cherokee history. It is performed in an outdoor amphitheater in the summer months.

Great Smoky Mountains Institute

The Great Smoky Mountains Institute is located at Tremont in the park and offers a wide variety of field seminars and workshops featuring everything from wildflower identification to photography.

Blue Ridge Parkway

The Blue Ridge Parkway is a linear national park that protects land along the 469-mile scenic highway. The road travels the top of the mountains from Rockfish Gap near Shenandoah National Park to the Oconaluftee River at the entrance to GSMNP. Nowhere else in the eastern United States can you travel such a distance almost completely surrounded by forest.

Sunrise over Blue Ridge Mountains from Blue Ridge Parkway.

Cherokee National Forest

The 627,000-acre national forest lies in Tennessee and borders GSMNP on both the east and the west. The forest boasts nine major rivers, 500 miles of hiking trails, and the 26-mile Ocoee River Scenic Byway. The forest has several wilderness areas where no motor vehicles are permitted. The 16,000-acre Citico Creek Wilderness is the largest in the forest. The two best white-water streams are the Hiwassee and the Ocoee, both popular with kayakers, rafters, and others. The John Muir Trail, named for the founder of the Sierra Club, follows 17 miles of the river corridor. Roan Mountain in the northern part of the forest features spectacular rhododendron blooms in June.

Nantahala National Forest

The 528,434-acre national forest borders GSMNP on the southwest. Portions of both the Appalachian Trail and Bartram Trail cross the forest. From 5,200-foot Wayah Bald, outstanding views of both Georgia and

Tennessee are possible. The forest features the Nantahala River, a famous white-water stream popular with kayakers and canoeists. Another river, the Cullasaja, has carved a spectacular gorge. The forest also has a number of spectacular waterfalls, including Cullasaja, Dry Falls, and the dramatic Whitewater Falls by Highlands, which tumbles 411 feet. One of the major features of the forest is the Joyce Kilmer Memorial Forest, boasting giant yellow poplars and other large trees, such as hemlock. The Joyce Kilmer–Slickrock Wilderness is another attraction.

Pisgah National Forest

The 504,863-acre Pisgah National Forest is nearly as large as GSMNP. The forest borders the northeast corner of the park and forms the border between North Carolina and Tennessee. It includes Mount Mitchell, which, at 6,684 feet, is the highest summit east of the Mississippi. The forest features 850 miles of trails, including the famed Appalachian Trail. The Black Mountains range has seventeen peaks above 6,000 feet. Black Mountain Trail, which begins on Mount Mitchell, provides access to this area of high peaks. The forest also features a number of wilderness areas, including Shining Rock, Linville Gorge, and Middle Prong. Pisgah shares Roan Mountain with adjacent Cherokee National Forest in Tennessee. Outstanding early-summer blooms of rhododendron can be seen there, as well as in the Craggy Mountains.

Wilderness Areas

The following brief descriptions provide an overview of some of the designated wilderness areas near GSMNP.

Citico Creek Wilderness (Tennessee)

The 16,000-acre Citico Creek Wilderness lies south of GSMNP in the Unicoi Mountains in Cherokee National Forest. It includes the upper headwaters of the Citico Creek watershed. Three major ridges slope away from the main crest of the range along the Tennessee–North Carolina border. The Citico is the largest wilderness area in Tennessee, with 58 miles of trails. The state line also serves as a boundary between the Citico Wilderness and the adjacent Joyce Kilmer–Slickrock Wilderness in North Carolina. Trails cross between both wilderness areas. Though the area has been logged, there are still stands of old-growth forest in remote places. Elevation varies from 1,400 to 4,600 feet.

Joyce Kilmer–Slickrock Wilderness
(North Carolina–Tennessee)

Most of the 17,013-acre Joyce Kilmer–Slickrock Wilderness lies in North Carolina in Nantahala National Forest, with some 3,832 acres in Cherokee National Forest in Tennessee. The wilderness borders the Citico Creek Wilderness in Tennessee. There are 60 miles of trails lacing this wild area, which includes Joyce Kilmer Memorial Forest, containing the best examples of large, old-growth hardwood forest in the eastern United States.

West Fork of Pigeon River in Middle Prong Wilderness, Pisgah National Forest.

An outcrop of white quartz gives the Shining Rocks Wilderness its name.

The drainages of the Little Santeetiah and Slickrock Creek watersheds are protected within the wilderness. Elevation ranges from 1,300 to 5,300 feet (Stratton Bald).

Middle Prong Wilderness (North Carolina)

The 7,900-acre Middle Prong Wilderness lies in Pisgah National Forest, to the east and north of GSMNP near Richland Balsam. It is nearly contiguous with Shining Rocks Wilderness, with only one road separating the two areas. Much of the area was logged, and the old logging railroad grades now serve as trails. Elevation ranges from 3,200 feet along the West Fork of the Pigeon River to 6,400 feet near Richland Balsam. The 6-mile-long Green Mountain Trail cross the area from north to south.

Shining Rocks Wilderness (North Carolina)

The 18,450-acre Shining Rocks Wilderness in Pisgah National Forest is named for Shining Rock Ledge, an outcrop of white quartz. It is accessible along the Blue Ridge Parkway. Elevation varies from 3,200 feet along the West Fork of the Pigeon River to 6,030 feet on Cold Mountain. There are a number of grassy balds in the wilderness, providing vistas. More than 25 miles of trail lace the wilderness. This wilderness is one of the most popular in North Carolina.

BIRD LIST

Loons and Grebes
___ Common Loon
(*Gavia immer*)
___ Horned Grebe
(*Podiceps auritus*)
___ Pied-billed Grebe
(*Podilymbus podiceps*)

**Storm-Petrels, Pelicans,
and Cormorants**
___ Band-rumped Storm-Petrel
(*Oceanodroma castro*)
___ American White Pelican
(*Pelecanus erthrorhynchos*)
___ Double-crested Cormorant
(*Phalacrocorax auritus*)

Herons, Bitterns, and Egrets
___ Great Blue Heron
(*Ardea herodias*)
___ American Bittern
(*Botaurus lentiginosus*)
___ Green Heron
(*Butorides virescens*)
___ Great Egret
(*Casmerodius albus*)
___ Little Blue Heron
(*Egretta caerulea*)

___ Least Bittern
(*Ixobrychus exilis*)
___ Yellow-crowned Night-Heron
(*Nyctanassa violacea*)
___ Black-crowned Night-Heron
(*Nycticorax nycticorax*)

Geese and Ducks
___ Wood Duck
(*Aix sponsa*)
___ Northern Pintail
(*Anas acuta*)
___ American Widgeon
(*Anas americana*)
___ Northern Shoveler
(*Anas clypeata*)
___ Green-winged Teal
(*Anas crecca*)
___ Blue-winged Teal
(*Anas discors*)
___ Mallard
(*Anas platyrhynchos*)
___ American Black Duck
(*Anas rubripes*)
___ Lesser Scaup
(*Aythya affinis*)
___ Ring-necked Duck
(*Aythya collaris*)

___ Brant
(*Branta bernicla*)
___ Canada Goose
(*Branta canadensis*)
___ Bufflehead
(*Bucephala albeola*)
___ Common Goldeneye
(*Bucephala clangula*)
___ Snow Goose
(*Chen caerulescens*)
___ Hooded Merganser
(*Lophodytes cucullatus*)
___ Common Merganser
(*Mergus merganser*)
___ Red-breasted Merganser
(*Mergus serrator*)

Vultures
___ Turkey Vulture
(*Cathartes aura*)
___ Black Vulture
(*Coragyps atratus*)

Hawks and Eagles
___ Cooper's Hawk
(*Accipiter cooperii*)
___ Northern Goshawk
(*Accipiter gentilis*)
___ Sharp-shinned Hawk
(*Accipiter striatus*)
___ Golden Eagle
(*Aquila chrysaetos*)
___ Red-tailed Hawk
(*Buteo jamaicensis*)
___ Red-shouldered Hawk
(*Buteo lineatus*)
___ Broad-winged Hawk
(*Buteo platypterus*)

___ Northern Harrier
(*Circus cyaneus*)
___ American Swallow-tailed Kite
(*Elanoides forficatus*)
___ Bald Eagle
(*Haliaeetus leucocephalus*)
___ Osprey
(*Pandion haliaetus*)

Falcons
___ Merlin
(*Falco columbarius*)
___ Peregrine Falcon
(*Falco peregrinus*)
___ American Kestrel
(*Falco sparverius*)

Grouse, Turkey, and Quail
___ Ruffed Grouse
(*Bonasa umbellus*)
___ Northern Bobwhite
(*Colinus virginianus*)
___ Wild Turkey
(*Meleagris gallopavo*)
___ Ring-necked Pheasant
(*Phasianus colchicus*)

Rails and Coots
___ American Coot
(*Fulica americana*)
___ Common Moorhen
(*Gallinula chloropus*)
___ Sora
(*Porzana carolina*)
___ King Rail
(*Rallus elegans*)
___ Virginia Rail
(*Rallus limicola*)

Cranes and Plovers
___ Killdeer
(*Charadrius vociferus*)
___ Sandhill Crane
(*Grus canadensis*)
___ Lesser Golden-Plover
(*Pluvialis dominica*)

Sandpipers and Phalaropes
___ Spotted Sandpiper
(*Actitis macularia*)
___ Semipalmated Sandpiper
(*Calidris pusilla*)
___ Common Snipe
(*Gallinago gallinago*)
___ Red Phalarope
(*Phalaropus fulicaria*)
___ Red-necked Phalarope
(*Phalaropus lobatus*)
___ Ruff
(*Philomachus pugnax*)
___ American Woodcock
(*Scolopax minor*)
___ Lesser Yellowlegs
(*Tringa flavipes*)
___ Greater Yellowlegs
(*Tringa melanoleuca*)
___ Solitary Sandpiper
(*Tringa solitaria*)

Gulls and Terns
___ Herring Gull
(*Larus argentatus*)
___ Laughing Gull
(*Larus atricilla*)
___ Ring-billed Gull
(*Larus delawarensis*)

___ Bonaparte's Gull
(*Larus philadelphia*)
___ Sooty Tern
(*Sterna fuscata*)

Cuckoos and Doves
___ Yellow-billed Cuckoo
(*Coccyzus americanus*)
___ Black-billed Cuckoo
(*Coccyzus erythropthalmus*)
___ Rock Dove
(*Columbia livia*)
___ Mourning Dove
(*Zenaida macroura*)

Owls
___ Northern Saw-whet Owl
(*Aegolius acadicus*)
___ Great Horned Owl
(*Bubo virginianus*)
___ Eastern Screech-Owl
(*Otus asio*)
___ Barred Owl
(*Strix varia*)
___ Barn Owl
(*Tyto alba*)

Nighthawks and Swifts
___ Chuck-will's-widow
(*Caprimulgus carolinensis*)
___ Whip-poor-will
(*Caprimulgus vociferus*)
___ Chimney Swift
(*Chaetura pelagica*)
___ Common Nighthawk
(*Chordeiles minor*)

Hummingbirds
___ Ruby-throated Hummingbird
(*Archilochus colubris*)

Kingfishers
___ Belted Kingfisher
(*Ceryle alcyon*)

Woodpeckers
___ Northern Flicker
(*Colaptes auratus*)
___ Pileated Woodpecker
(*Dryocopus pileatus*)
___ Red-bellied Woodpecker
(*Melanerpes carolinus*)
___ Red-headed Woodpecker
(*Melanerpes erythrocephalus*)
___ Red-cockaded Woodpecker
(*Picoides borealis*)
___ Downy Woodpecker
(*Picoides pubescens*)
___ Hairy Woodpecker
(*Picoides villosus*)
___ Yellow-bellied Sapsucker
(*Sphyrapicus varius*)

Flycatchers
___ Olive-sided Flycatcher
(*Contopus cooperi*)
___ Eastern Wood Pewee
(*Contopus virens*)
___ Alder Flycatcher
(*Empidonax alnorum*)
___ Yellow-bellied Flycatcher
(*Empidonax flaviventris*)
___ Least Flycatcher
(*Empidonax minimus*)

___ Willow Flycatcher
(*Empidonax trailii*)
___ Acadian Flycatcher
(*Empidonax virescens*)
___ Great Crested Flycatcher
(*Myiarchus crinitus*)
___ Eastern Phoebe
(*Sayornis phoebe*)
___ Eastern Kingbird
(*Tyrannus tyrannus*)
___ Western Kingbird
(*Tyrannus verticalis*)

Larks
___ Horned Lark
(*Eremophila alpestris*)

Swallows
___ Cliff Swallow
(*Hirundo pyrrhonota*)
___ Barn Swallow
(*Hirundo rustica*)
___ Purple Martin
(*Progne subis*)
___ Bank Swallow
(*Riparia riparia*)
___ Northern Rough-winged
Swallow
(*Stelgidopteryx serripennis*)
___ Tree Swallow
(*Tachycineta bicolor*)

Crows, Ravens, and Jays
___ American Crow
(*Corvus brachyrhynchos*)
___ Common Raven
(*Corvus corax*)

____ Blue Jay
(*Cyanocitta cristata*)

Chickadees and Nuthatches
____ Tufted Titmouse
(*Baeolophus bicolor*)
____ Brown Creeper
(*Certhia americana*)
____ Black-capped Chickadee
(*Poecile atricapillus*)
____ Carolina Chickadee
(*Poecile carolinensis*)
____ Red-breasted Nuthatch
(*Sitta canadensis*)
____ White-breasted Nuthatch
(*Sitta carolinensis*)

Wrens
____ Marsh Wren
(*Cistothorus palustris*)
____ Sedge Wren
(*Cistothorus platensia*)
____ Bewick's Wren
(*Thryomanes bewickii*)
____ Carolina Wren
(*Thryothorus ludovicianus*)
____ House Wren
(*Troglodytes aedon*)
____ Winter Wren
(*Troglodytes troglodytes*)

Gnatcatchers and Kinglets
____ Blue-gray Gnatcatcher
(*Polioptila caerulea*)
____ Ruby-crowned Kinglet
(*Regulus calendula*)
____ Golden-crowned Kinglet
(*Regulus satrapa*)

Thrushes
____ Veery
(*Catharus fuscescens*)
____ Hermit Thrush
(*Catharus guttatus*)
____ Gray-cheeked Thrush
(*Catharus minimus*)
____ Swainson's Thrush
(*Catharus ustulatus*)
____ Wood Thrush
(*Hylocichla mustelina*)
____ Eastern Bluebird
(*Sialia sialis*)
____ American Robin
(*Turdus migratorius*)

Mockingbirds and Thrashers
____ Gray Catbird
(*Dumetella carolinensis*)
____ Northern Mockingbird
(*Mimus polyglottos*)
____ Brown Thrasher
(*Toxostoma rufum*)

Pipits, Waxwings, and Shrikes
____ American Pipit
(*Anthus rubescens*)
____ Cedar Waxwing
(*Bombycilla cedrorum*)
____ Loggerhead Shrike
(*Lanius ludovicianus*)

Starlings
____ European Starling
(*Sturnus vulgaris*)

Vireos

___ Yellow-throated Vireo
(*Vireo flavifrons*)

___ Warbling Vireo
(*Vireo gilvus*)

___ White-eyed Vireo
(*Vireo griseus*)

___ Red-eyed Vireo
(*Vireo olivaceus*)

___ Philadelphia Vireo
(*Vireo philadelphicus*)

___ Blue-headed Vireo
(*Vireo solitarius*)

Warblers

___ Black-throated Blue Warbler
(*Dendroica caerulescens*)

___ Bay-breasted Warbler
(*Dendroica castanea*)

___ Cerulean Warbler
(*Dendroica cerulea*)

___ Yellow-rumped Warbler
(*Dendroica coronata*)

___ Prairie Warbler
(*Dendroica discolor*)

___ Yellow-throated Warbler
(*Dendroica dominica*)

___ Blackburnian Warbler
(*Dendroica fusca*)

___ Magnolia Warbler
(*Dendroica magnolia*)

___ Palm Warbler
(*Dendroica palmarum*)

___ Chestnut-sided Warbler
(*Dendroica pensylvanica*)

___ Yellow Warbler
(*Dendroica petechia*)

___ Pine Warbler
(*Dendroica pinus*)

___ Blackpoll Warbler
(*Dendroica straita*)

___ Cape May Warbler
(*Dendroica tigrina*)

___ Black-throated Green Warbler
(*Dendroica virens*)

___ Common Yellowthroat
(*Geothlypis trichas*)

___ Worm-eating Warbler
(*Helmitheros vermivorus*)

___ Yellow-breasted Chat
(*Icteria virens*)

___ Swainson's Warbler
(*Limnothlypis swainsonii*)

___ Black-and-white Warbler
(*Mniotilta varia*)

___ Kentucky Warbler
(*Oporornis formosus*)

___ Northern Parula
(*Parula americana*)

___ Prothonotary Warbler
(*Protonotaria citrea*)

___ Ovenbird
(*Seiurus aurocapillus*)

___ Louisiana Waterthrush
(*Seiurus motacilla*)

___ Northern Waterthrush
(*Seiurus noveboracensis*)

___ American Redstart
(*Setophaga ruticilla*)

___ Orange-crowned Warbler
(*Vermivora celata*)

___ Golden-winged Warbler
(*Vermivora chrysoptera*)

___ Tennessee Warbler
(*Vermivora peregrina*)

___ Blue-winged Warbler
(*Vermivora pinus*)
___ Nashville Warbler
(*Vermivora ruficapilla*)
___ Canada Warbler
(*Wilsonia canadensis*)
___ Hooded Warbler
(*Wilsonia citrina*)
___ Wilson's Warbler
(*Wilsonia pusilla*)

Tanagers
___ Scarlet Tanager
(*Piranga olivacea*)
___ Summer Tanager
(*Piranga rubra*)

Cardinals
___ Northern Cardinal
(*Cardinalis cardinalis*)
___ Blue Grosbeak
(*Guiraca caerulea*)
___ Indigo Bunting
(*Passerina cyanea*)
___ Rose-breasted Grosbeak
(*Pheucticus ludovicianus*)
___ Dickcissel
(*Spiza americana*)

Sparrows
___ Backman's Sparrow
(*Aimophila aestivalis*)
___ Henslow's Sparrow
(*Ammodramus henslowii*)
___ Le Conte's Sparrow
(*Ammodramus leconteii*)
___ Grasshopper Sparrow
(*Ammodramus savannarum*)

___ Lark Sparrow
(*Chondestes grammacus*)
___ Dark-eyed Junco
(*Junco hyemalis*)
___ Swamp Sparrow
(*Melospiza georgiana*)
___ Lincoln's Sparrow
(*Melospiza lincolnii*)
___ Song Sparrow
(*Melospiza melodia*)
___ Savannah Sparrow
(*Passerculus sandwichensis*)
___ Fox Sparrow
(*Passerella iliaca*)
___ Eastern Towhee
(*Pipilo erythrophthalmus*)
___ Snow Bunting
(*Plectrophenax nivalis*)
___ Vesper Sparrow
(*Pooecetes gramineus*)
___ Chipping Sparrow
(*Spizella passerina*)
___ Field Sparrow
(*Spizella pusilla*)
___ White-throated Sparrow
(*Zonotrichia albicollis*)
___ White-crowned Sparrow
(*Zonotrichia leucophrys*)

Blackbirds
___ Red-winged Blackbird
(*Agelaius phoeniceus*)
___ Bobolink
(*Dolichonyx oryzivorus*)
___ Rusty Blackbird
(*Euphagus carolinus*)
___ Northern Oriole
(*Icterus galbula*)

___ Orchard Oriole
   (*Icterus spurius*)
___ Brown-headed Cowbird
   (*Molothrus ater*)
___ Common Grackle
   (*Quiscalus quiscula*)
___ Eastern Meadowlark
   (*Sturnella magna*)

Finches and Crossbills
___ Common Redpoll
   (*Carduelis flammea*)
___ Pine Siskin
   (*Carduelis pinus*)
___ American Goldfinch
   (*Carduelis tristis*)

___ House Finch
   (*Carpodacus mexicanus*)
___ Purple Finch
   (*Carpodacus purpureus*)
___ Evening Grosbeak
   (*Coccothraustes verpertinus*)
___ Red Crossbill
   (*Loxia curvirostra*)
___ White-winged Crossbill
   (*Loxia leucoptera*)

Old World Sparrows
___ House Sparrow
   (*Passer domesticus*)

Index

Page numbers in italics indicate illustrations or photographs.